D0604271

THE HUMAN VOLCANO

THE HUMAN VOLCANO

POPULATION GROWTH AS GEOLOGIC FORCE

The Changing Earth Series

JON ERICKSON

AN INFOBASE HOLDINGS COMPANY

THE HUMAN VOLCANO: POPULATION GROWTH AS GEOLOGIC FORCE

Facts On File, Inc.
460 Park Avenue South
New York NY 10016

Library of Congress Cataloging-in-Publication Data

Erickson, Jon, 1948–
The human volcano: population growth as geologic force / Jon Erickson.
p. cm. — (The changing earth series)
Includes bibliographical references and index.
ISBN 0-8160-3130-4 (acid-free paper)
1. Man—Influence on nature. 2. Population. 3. Environmental degradation. I. Series: Erickson, Jon, 1948– Changing earth.
GF75.E75 1995
304.2—dc20 94–32148

Text design by Ron Monteleone/Robert Yaffe
Jacket design by Catherine Rincon Hyman
Printed in the United States of America

RRD FOF 10 9 8 7 6 5 4 3 2 1

This book is printed on acid-free paper.

CONTENTS

TABLES

ACKNOWLEDGMENTS

The author thanks the following organizations for providing photographs for this book: the National Aeronautics and Space Administration (NASA), the National Center for Atmospheric Research (NCAR), the National Oceanic and Atmospheric Administration (NOAA), the National Park Service, the U.S. Army Corps of Engineers, the U.S. Department of Agriculture (USDA), the USDA–Forest Service, the USDA–Soil Conservation Service, the U.S. Defense Nuclear Agency, the U.S. Department of Defense, the U.S. Department of Energy, the U.S. Geological Survey (USGS), and the U.S. Navy.

INTRODUCTION

The human race came into being during a time of high species diversity—perhaps the greatest diversity in the history of the Earth. Today, however, the world is losing valuable plant and animal species at an alarming rate because of burgeoning human populations crowding into their environments. Our rapid population growth is inflicting major damage on the Earth, as people encroach into wildlife habitats in a desperate struggle for survival. If present trends of environmental destruction continue to spiral out of control, the planet could tumble into cataclysmic extinction.

We are called the "human volcano" because our effects on the environment are global—like major volcanic eruptions. Such convulsions have been cited as causes of mass extinctions of species throughout the Earth's history. However, the extinctions of the past occurred on geologic time scales and not compressed into a mere century, as in modern times. The numbers of species disappearing today far exceeds the natural rate of extinction prior to the arrival of humans. High human population growth with its rising demands on the environment and increasing pollution threatens to transform the planet in a manner comparable to the effects of long-term geologic forces.

Dramatic changes are occurring globally, and humans appear to be responsible for the deteriorating condition of the planet. We are damaging the Earth by improper use of land and water resources, large-scale extraction and combustion of fossil fuels, widespread pollution of the environment with industrial and agricultural poisons, and global destruction of wildlife habitats. These activities are also interfering with the Earth's critical cycles and disrupting the balance of nature. Our uncontrolled population explosion places us in the unique position of causing widespread environmental destruction in a comparably short period. We thus constitute a major geologic force on the face of the Earth, and it remains to be seen what kind of world will result from our folly.

Our species is conducting a dangerous global experiment by cramming as many people as possible onto the planet. We are altering the environment with our waste products, destroying the forests, and pumping pollutants into the air and water, thus unfavorably changing the composition of the biosphere and interfering with the Earth's energy balance.

Human activities appear to be responsible for many of the climatic disturbances that beset the planet. The gaseous composition of the atmosphere has changed significantly faster than at any other time in human history. Global warming from man-made greenhouse gases could radically alter the climate, spawning deadly storms that could bring much death and destruction. Changing climatic conditions could also turn large parts of the world into desolate wastelands, sharply curtailing agricultural productivity at a time when it is needed most. A deadly combination of drought, disease, and infestation could conspire against humanity, causing massive famine and death.

The human race is on a collision course, caught between limited natural resources and the rising numbers of people demanding them. Rapid population growth is stretching the resources of the world, and the prospect of future increases raises doubts whether the planet can continue to support people's growing needs. The increase in world economic activity that will be needed to keep pace with rising human requirements could subject the biosphere to conditions it cannot possibly tolerate without irreversible damage. The depletion of natural resources could also jeopardize further human advancement and lead to violent armed conflicts that would undoubtedly take a great many lives.

Populations are growing so explosively, and modifying the environment so extensively, that we are producing global change of unprecedented dimensions. With more people in the world, more forests are cleared, more firewood is gathered, more topsoil is eroded, and more pollution is created. Every ton of carbon dioxide, every gallon of pollution, and every extinction of species brings the world closer to a habitability crisis. The slow strangulation of the Earth inevitably makes habitation difficult for humankind as well as for the rest of the living world. As populations continue to grow out of control and lay waste the land, the human race can expect many unpleasant surprises.

1

THE DAWN OF CIVILIZATION

At Laetoli, Tanzania, a well-preserved set of footprints was found in 1977 embedded in a volcanic ash bed called the Footprint Tuff. The footprints had been made about 3.7 million years ago, and the feet that made them apparently had rounded heels, uplifted arches, pronounced balls, and forward-pointing toes—all marks of an efficient mode of locomotion. In addition, the tracks clearly showed that their owner preferred walking on two legs. Astonishingly, these fossil footprints were made by our earliest ancestors, walking upright nearly 2 million years prior to the use of tools.

The development of a bipedal mode of walking marked the beginning of the human line. It was a major contributor to human evolution, freeing the hands for useful tasks and cooling the body in the hot savanna by exposing it to cool breezes. Early humans were probably highly mobile scavengers, following migrating herds of animals over long distances. Bipedal walking was also necessary for covering large territories to forage for plant foods. Stiff competition drove the need for tool-making, necessary for successful habitation in a harsh environment, and another strong force in human evolution.

THE HUMAN LINE

Primates evolved more than 50 million years ago from a small squirrel-like mammal. The primate family tree split into two branches, with monkeys on one branch and apes on the other. The ape line includes the hominoids, our ancient humanlike ancestors. Approximately 30 million years ago, the precursors of apes lived most of their lives in the dense tropical rain forests of Egypt, which today is mostly desert. These apelike ancestors spread from Africa into Europe and Asia between 25 and 10 million years ago (Fig. 1-1). The Eurasian climate was one of seasonal changes, with mild winters. What is now grassland and desert were then woodlands and forests, which were much more widespread than they are today.

The split between African and Asian apes coincided with the collision of the landmasses of Africa-Arabia and Eurasia some 17 million years ago. The linkup of the two landmasses sparked the migration of African hominoids along with other mammals into the rest of the Old World. The contact between the continents also initiated a major mountain-building episode that raised the Alps and other ranges in Europe and eliminated the Tethys Sea, which linked the Indian and Atlantic oceans. At that time, the climates of Europe and Asia were warmer and the forests were lusher than they are now.

The African apes, including gorillas and chimpanzees, are more closely related to humans than the Asian apes, the orangutans and gibbons. The

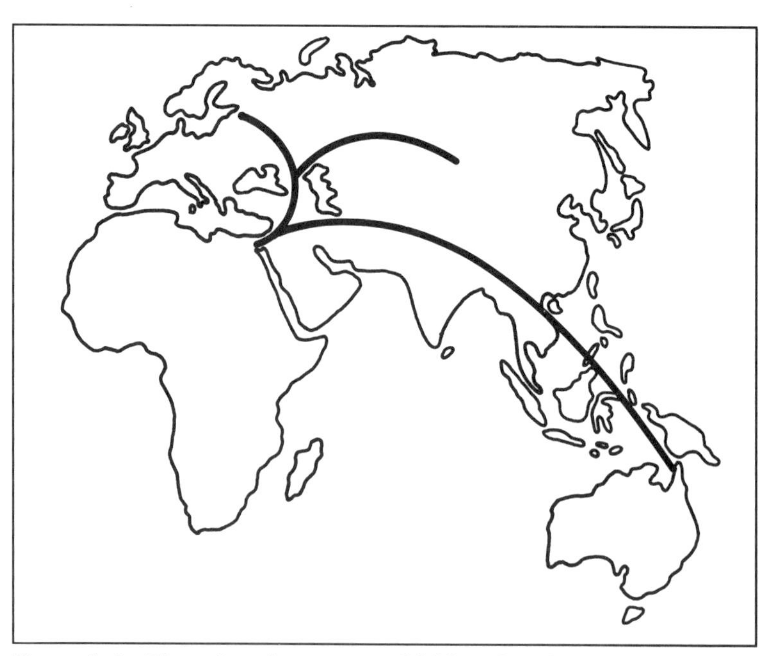

Figure 1–1 The migration routes of African hominoids.

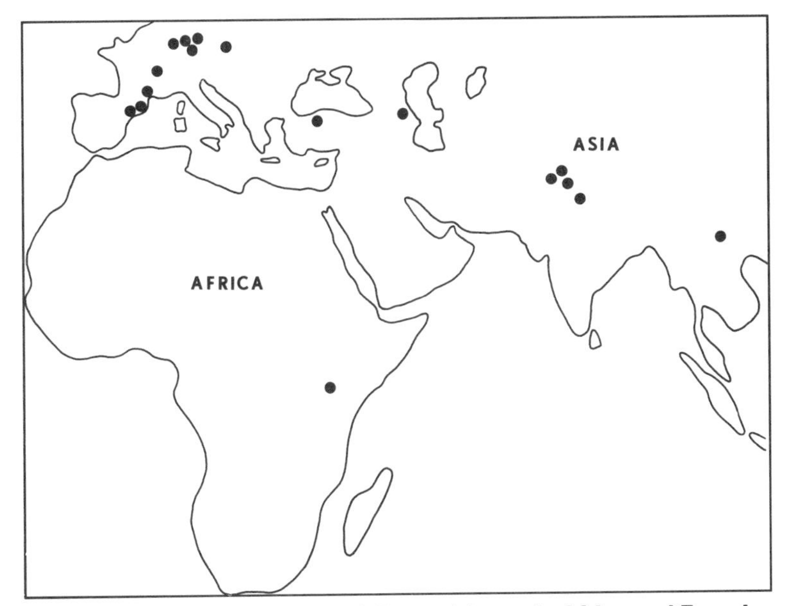

Figure 1–2 The distribution of *Ramapithecus* in Africa and Eurasia.

radiation of the great apes from an ancestral stock occurred around 15 million years ago. These earlier large hominoids were highly diverse, though only five genera have survived to the present. The common ancestor of apes and humans is thought to be an apelike creature called *Proconsul,* which was about the size of a baboon and lived from about 22 to 16 million years ago. It was a tree-dwelling, fruit-eating animal that walked mainly on all fours, and males were distinctly larger than females. *Proconsul* evolved after monkeys became a separate branch of the primate family tree but before chimpanzees, gorillas, orangutans, and hominids branched off.

Between 12 and 9 million years ago, the forests of Europe were home to a tree-living, fruit-eating ape called *Dryopithecus,* which probably gave rise to *Ramapithecus* (Fig. 1-2), an early hominoid with more advanced characteristics than earlier hominoids. These features have led to speculation that *Ramapithecus* was an early hominid and that the hominids diverged from the African hominoids at least 15 million years ago. However, *Ramapithecus* appears to be more closely related to the sole surviving Asian great ape, the orangutan. Between 9 and 4 million years ago, the fossil record jumps from the hominidlike but mainly ape form of *Ramapithecus* to the true hominids (Fig. 1-3).

THE ORIGIN OF HUMANS

Possibly as early as 9 million years ago, the hominids evolved in Africa from an ancestor they had in common with the gorilla and chimpanzee—

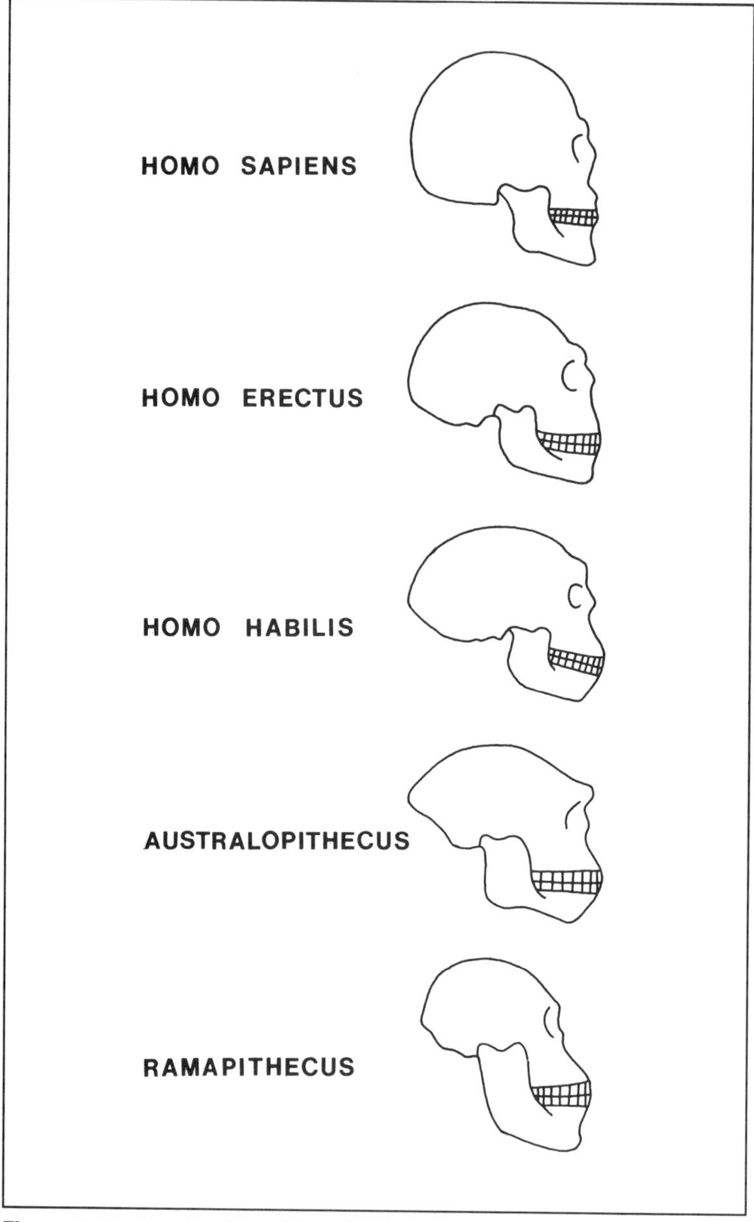

Figure 1–3 Hominoid and hominid skulls.

the latter of which shares about 99 percent of its genetic makeup with humans. Around 7 million years ago, much of Africa became cooler and drier; forests retreated and were replaced with grasslands. Life on the savanna, where our ancient ancestors roamed, was harsher than life in the forests, where the chimpanzees lived. In order to survive under adverse conditions, early humans rapidly evolved into an intelligent, upright-walking species, whereas the chimpanzees, whose environment was less challenging, are much the same today as they were several million years ago.

The development of permanent bipedal walking and running, which set the hands free for carrying objects, for tool-making, and for other useful tasks, played a fundamental role in human evolution. The rapid evolution from an apelike to a more human form might have resulted from violent conflicts between different tribes, in much the same way chimpanzees attack neighboring bands. These violent conflicts might have been a strong driving force behind early human advancement, as they have been in historic times.

An early hominid species called *Australopithecus* (Fig. 1-4) first appeared about 4 million years ago in Tanzania and Ethiopia and perhaps a million years earlier in northern Kenya. A half complete skeleton of an adult female named Lucy was discovered in 1974 at Hadar, Ethiopia and dated between 3 and 3.6 million years old. These hominids were markedly different from modern humans: The skull of some specimens contained a prominent bony crest that ran over the top and down the back (Fig. 1-5), presumably for anchoring powerful jaw muscles used for gnawing tough foods, or to transform the mouth into a "third hand." They walked on two legs but retained many apelike features, such as arms that were long relative to their legs, and curved bones in their hands and feet to enable them to take refuge in trees.

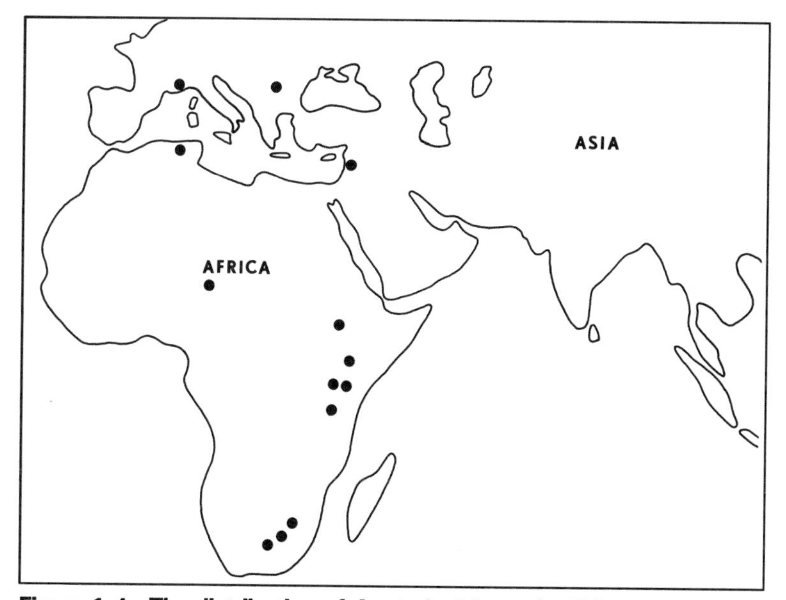

Figure 1–4 The distribution of *Australopithecus* in Africa and Eurasia.

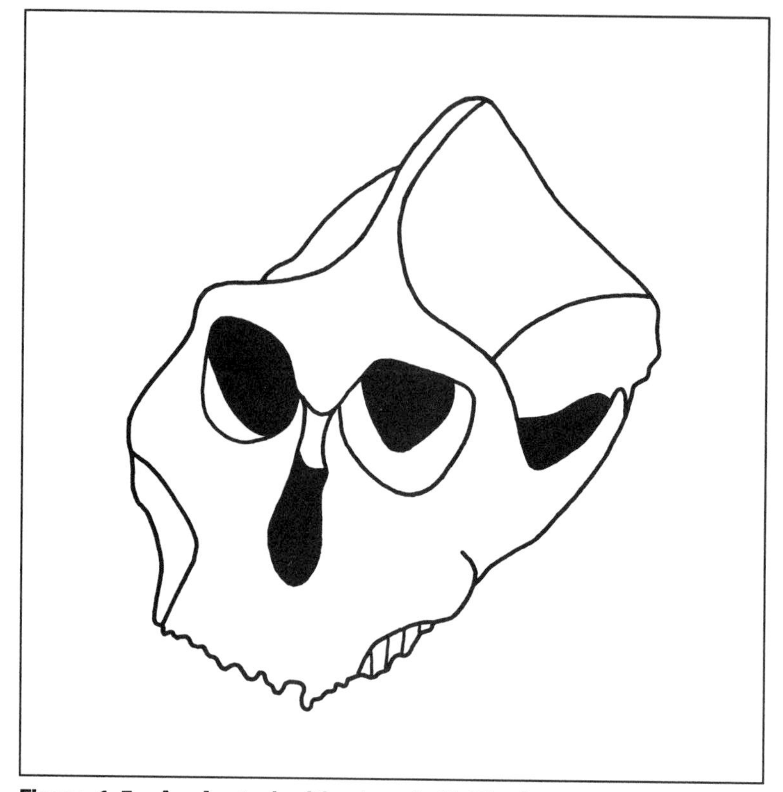

Figure 1–5 An Australopithecine skull. The large ridge crest supported massive jaw muscles.

They were quite muscular—much stronger than modern humans. The average male stood a little less than 5 feet tall and weighed about 100 pounds, the female about 4 feet tall and about 70 pounds. The exaggerated size difference between the sexes is a characteristic typical of early human species and is known as sexual dimorphism. It probably resulted from sharp competition among males for females, as seen in the behavior of gorillas today. With more cooperation among males as hominids evolved from a scavenging to a hunting way of life, sexual dimorphism became less pronounced.

Two or more lines of Australopithecine existed simultaneously in Africa and survived practically unchanged for more than a million years. After a lengthy period of apparent stability, all but one line became extinct, possibly due to a changing climate or habitat. The gracile (thin-boned) Australopithecines, represented by Lucy and a 2-million-year-old, well-preserved skull of a child found in the Taung region of southeast Africa, apparently gave rise to the *Homo* line of hominids.

THE LOWER PALEOLITHIC

About 2.5 million years ago, global temperatures fell, initiating a series of ice ages. The climate change produced a shift toward more open, savannalike habitats in Africa, resulting in the appearance of many new animal species and spurring the evolution of early humans. During this time, there might have been several species of African hominids living in the same area. Their small brain size indicates that early humans did not have the prolonged period of juvenile dependency that allows modern children to develop their mental abilities. Early childhood was extremely difficult, and high infant mortality kept the populations of some hominid species small, while other species declined and eventually went extinct.

A larger-brained hominid called *Homo habilis* ("handy man") evolved in Africa about 2 million years ago (Fig. 1-6). *Homo habilis* is classified as the first species of true humans and appears to mark a transition between apelike and humanlike hominids. The species was much like *Australopithecus* in its face and teeth, but it had a significantly larger brain, averaging about 700 cubic centimeters, or about half the size of modern human brains. The limb bones were markedly different from those of *Australopithecus,* resembling those of later human species. *Homo habilis* was the first human species to make and use tools regularly, hence its name. It also had well-developed speech centers, indicating a language capability.

Around 1.8 million years ago. *Homo habilis* disappeared from Africa and was replaced by *Homo erectus.* This species is widely accepted as human and appears to have evolved from *Homo habilis* in Africa, although it might

TABLE 1–1 HUMAN CULTURAL EVOLUTION

Date (in years ago)	Event
2,000,000	Appearance of *Homo habilis* and of tool-making
300,000	Appearance of Neanderthal
100,000	Appearance of Cro-Magnon (*Homo sapiens sapiens*)
32,000	Appearance of the flute
29,000	Appearance of cave art
27,000	Appearance of Venus figures
23,000	Appearance of sewing needles
17,000	Appearance of spear-throwers
12,000	Appearance of bows and arrows
10,000	Beginning of civilization

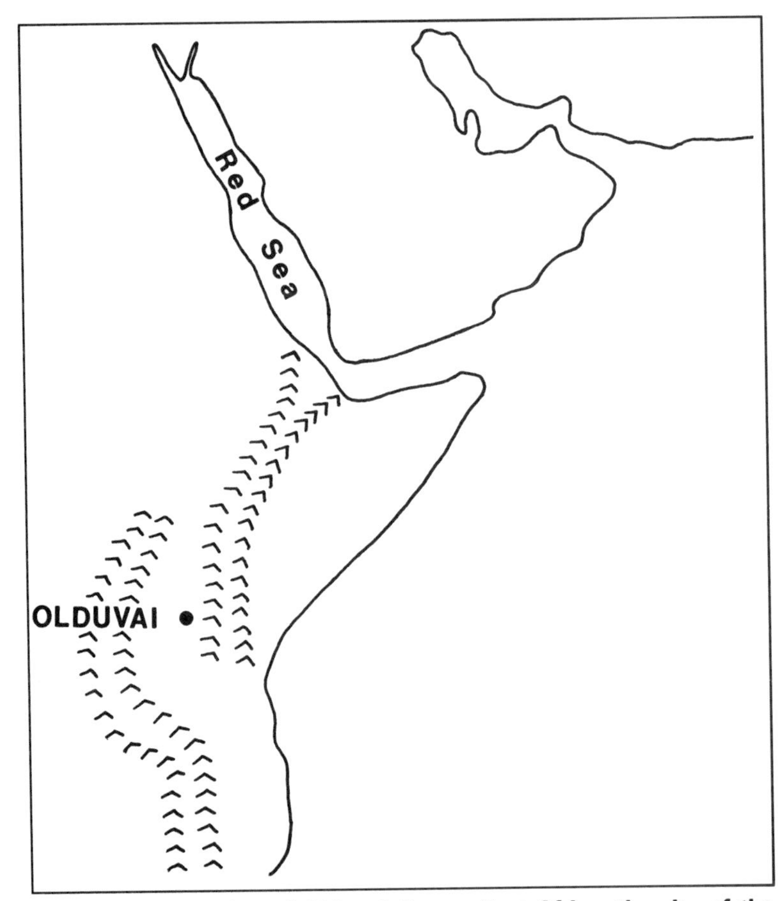

Figure 1–6 Location of Olduvai Gorge, East Africa, the site of the discovery of 1.8-million-year-old *Homo habilis* bones.

have evolved in Asia independently of *Homo habilis* and subsequently migrated to Africa. A large modification in body form indicates a spurt of evolutionary growth from *Homo habilis* to *Homo erectus,* the latter of which shared many attributes of modern humans. Sexual dimorphism, which was extreme in *Homo habilis*—males were about twice as large as females—was greatly diminished in *Homo erectus.* Its brain was also larger than that of *Homo habilis,* measuring about 1,000 cubic centimeters—about two-thirds the size of modern human brains.

About 1 million years ago, *Homo erectus* occupied southern and eastern Asia (Fig. 1-7), where the species lived until about 200,000 years ago. These people developed an elaborate culture, inhabiting caves and hunting game. They were probably the first people to develop an advanced form of communication, which enabled them to organize hunting parties and to pass down tool-making skills to the next generation.

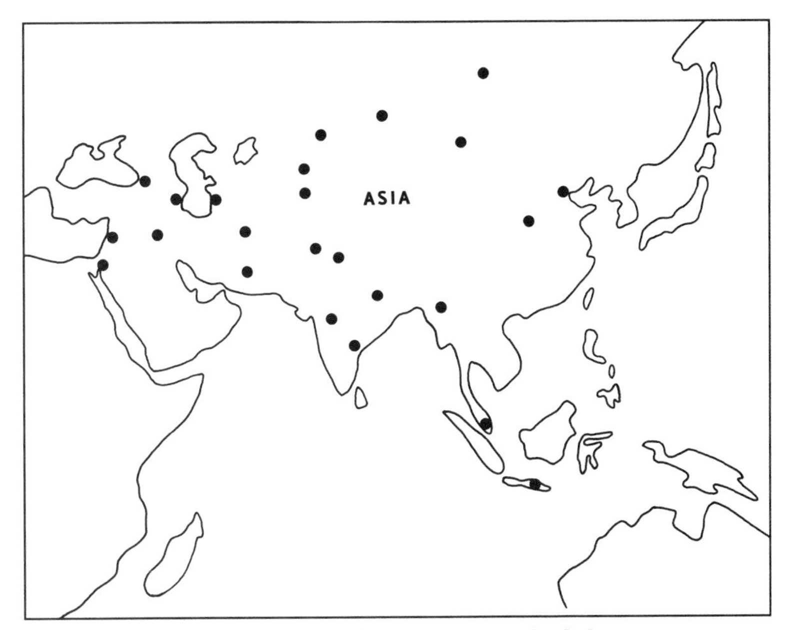

Figure 1–7 The distribution of *Homo erectus* in Asia.

Some populations of *Homo erectus* might have been the first to use fire. People discovered fire possibly as early as 800,000 years ago—fortunately for the future of humans, because without it they might not have survived the cold glacial periods in the northern latitudes. Whether humans could ignite a fire by this time is uncertain; most likely, they simply utilized fires that were naturally set by lightning strikes. For thousands of years, people used fire for cooking, for heating, and for hunting game—setting brushfires to frighten animals into running into traps or stampeding off cliffs.

Peking man was a variety of *Homo erectus* that lived in China from about 400,000 to 200,000 years ago. Another variety, called Java man, left the Asian continent and arrived in Java about 700,000 years ago. About 60,000 years ago, the descendants of Java man migrated to Australia, where they apparently evolved into modern Aborigines. Many other types of *Homo erectus* were scattered over the world. It therefore appears that anatomically modern humans might have evolved from *Homo erectus* not just in Africa but in several places, possibly accounting for differences in races among modern humans.

The Neanderthals, a species of *Homo sapiens,* first appeared about 300,000 years ago. They are named for the Neander Valley near Dusseldorf, Germany, where the first fossils were discovered in 1856. The Neanderthals are generally thought to have been cave dwellers, but they also sometimes occupied open-air sites, as indicated by hearths and rings made of mammoth bones and the masses of stone tools typically associated with these people. They might have made rock carvings and cave paintings, and they appear to have buried their dead, placing offerings such as ibex horns and flowers in the graves.

Evidence suggests that the Neanderthals might have practiced cannibalism. In Italy's Guattari Cave, where Neanderthals lived between 100,000 and 50,000 years ago, an adult male skull was found ringed by stones from an apparent ritual of cannibalism. Such skull bones might have been kept as trophies or ritual objects. Human bones found at a cave in the former Yugoslavia have long been viewed as the remains of a cannibal feast more than 50,000 years ago. What appears to be human cannibalism has emerged at other sites, including a cave in France where 60,000-year-old bones were found. It is not clear whether cannibalism was practiced routinely and systematically or only in rare cases of imminent starvation.

During the last interglacial period, called the Eemian, about 130,000 years ago, the Neanderthals ranged over most of western Europe and central Asia (Fig. 1-8) and extended as far north as the Arctic Ocean. They thrived in these regions until about 30,000 years ago, apparently becoming extinct over a period of perhaps 5,000 years. The Neanderthals' great success is illustrated by their ability to endure the rigors of the cold climate during the last ice age from about 100,000 to 10,000 years ago. The Neanderthals' massive muscles, used during hunting and other activities, probably supplied their bulky bodies with the heat needed to survive the bitter cold conditions.

Neanderthal babies were apparently larger than those of modern humans and were perhaps born after a longer gestation period—an adaptation that might have been required for the infants' survival in cold climates. Other

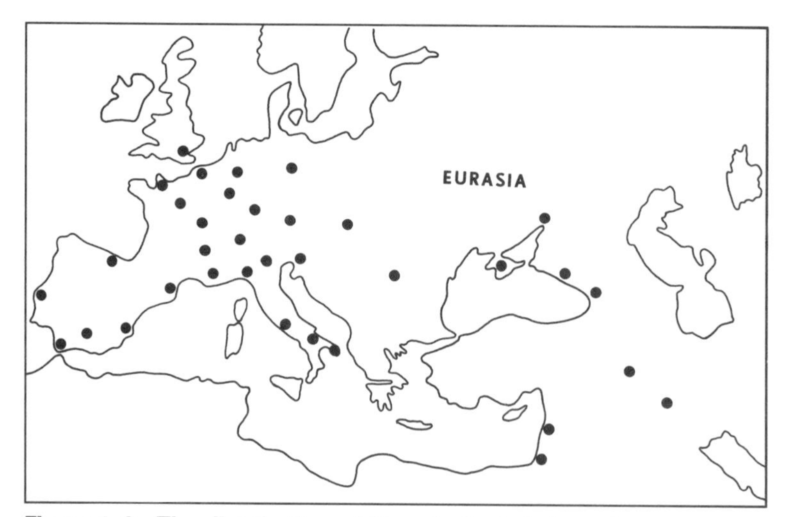

Figure 1–8 The distribution of Neanderthals in Eurasia.

physical attributes such as a thick layer of subcutaneous fat might have been adaptations to the cold subarctic, resembling those exhibited by modern Inuits and Lapps. The Neanderthals' brain size, which was generally larger than that of anatomically modern humans, is also attributed to their bulkier bodies.

The sudden disappearance of the Neanderthals after over 100,000 years of prosperity might have resulted from their assimilation by a more advanced species of homo sapiens known as Cro-Magnon. These early modern humans were named for the Cro-Magnon cave in France, where the first discoveries were made in 1868. Their evolutionary line can be traced back to Africa, perhaps 250,000 years ago. However, evidence also suggests that

Figure 1–9 Comparison of the mammoth (top) and the mastodon (bottom), both of which went extinct at the end of the last ice age.

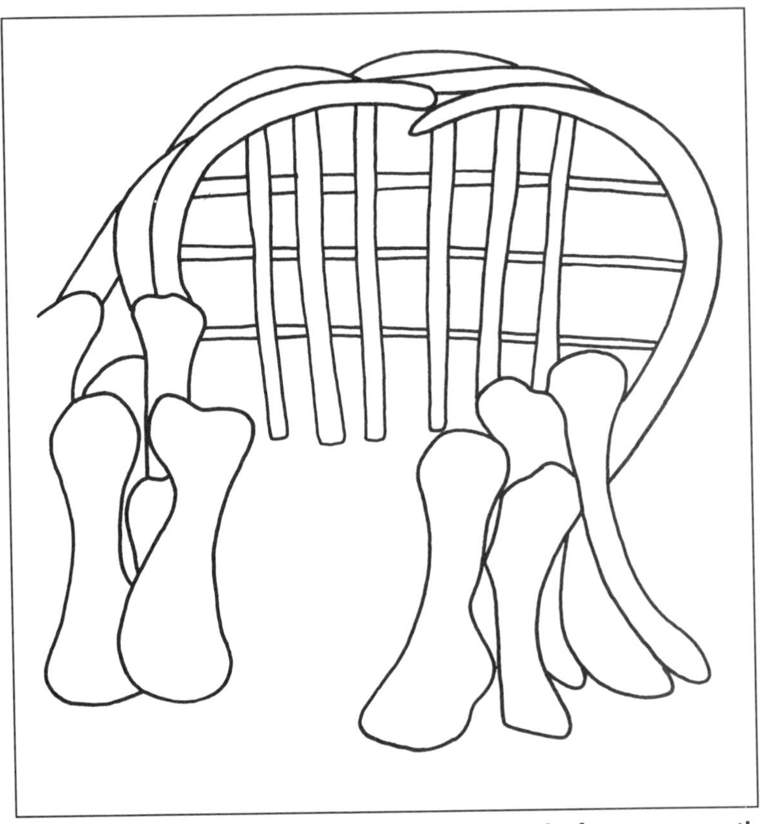

Figure 1–10 A primitive arctic dwelling made from mammoth bones.

they arose simultaneously in several parts of the world, as long ago as 1 million years, possibly evolving from *Homo erectus.* Neanderthals and modern humans apparently coexisted in Eurasia for at least 60,000 years and shared many of the same cultural advancements, although with probably little or no interbreeding. Furthermore, neither species appears to have been more intelligent than the other.

Physically, the Cro-Magnon were markedly different from the Neanderthals and shared most of the physical attributes of humans living today. Their cranial capacity was as large as ours, and their brain case proportions were modern in structure. The skull was short, high, and rounded, without the Neanderthal's large brow ridges and pronounced bony bump at the back of the skull. The face was robust and flat like that of modern Europeans, and the lower jaw ended in a definite chin. The skeleton was slender and long-limbed in contrast to the stocky Neanderthals.

Sometime during the last ice age, the Cro-Magnon advanced into Europe and Asia, probably during a warm interlude when the climate was not so severe. These people might have been attracted into such desolate, frozen wastelands by a rich stock of large animals. The European landscape at this time was largely grassland. On this range roamed reindeer, woolly mammoths, and mastodons (Fig. 1-9), along with other species specially adapted to the cold. The Cro-Magnon hunted these animals extensively and carved up their carcasses with finely honed stone blades. Deadly spears, often engraved with animal images, were effective weapons for hunting big game.

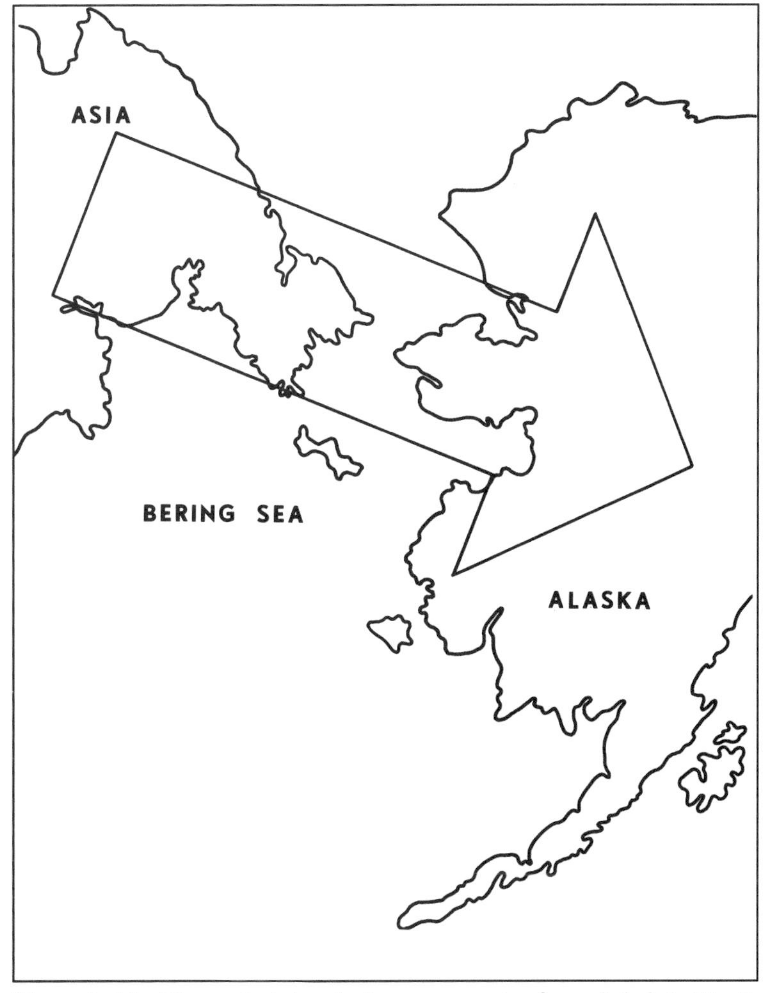

Figure 1–11 The route taken by ice age peoples from Asia into North America via the Bering Strait.

The slaughter might have led to the extinction of certain species that were easy prey to the Cro-Magnons' advanced hunting skills.

These ice age peoples probably lived much like present-day natives of the arctic tundra. They fished the rivers, possibly using small boats, and hunted reindeer and other animals. Due to the scarcity of wood in the cold tundra, ice age hunters of the central Russian plain built houses out of mammoth bones and tusks covered with animal hides (Fig. 1-10) and burned bones and animal fat for heat and light. Changes in population sizes were often dramatic in these regions, and some human populations in the Northern Hemisphere shrank because of climate fluctuations.

People populated the Americas at least 30,000 years ago by crossing a land bridge between Siberia and Alaska during the last ice age (Fig. 1-11), when sea levels dropped several hundred feet and exposed ocean platforms. Rather than migrating to North America in several waves, however, small bands of nomadic hunters probably crossed the ancient land bridges in pursuit of game and ended up on the new continent by accident. The human hunters arriving from Asia sped across the virgin continent following migrating herds of large herbivores. The early Native Americans then crossed over the Panama isthmus into South America and roamed as far as southern Chile.

The peopling of the Pacific took place when sea levels dropped during the last ice age, exposing island chains, which allowed a human migration of immense proportions. Humans occupied the continent of Australia as early as 60,000 years ago. By island-hopping from southeast Asia, Polynesian people settled the great ocean reaches, possibly traveling as far east as South America.

THE UPPER PALEOLITHIC

The Upper Paleolithic, between 35,000 and 10,000 years ago, is synonymous with the emergence of truly modern humans, and of an advanced culture. The period witnessed an explosion of human progress and creativity that serves as a milestone in human development. Humans made more technological and artistic advances during this time than in the entire preceding 2 million years. In a quantum leap forward, people invented elaborate forms of language, art, and music. They also laid down the foundations for laws, trade, class distinctions, and fashion.

Late ice age peoples made elaborate and beautiful drawings and carvings of animals they held in high regard, such as horses and cave bears. They invented sewing needles to tailor cold-weather clothing needed for colonizing the colder regions of Europe. They buried their dead and adorned

Figure 1–12 Cave drawings, like this buffalo, often represented animals early humans respected and hunted.

the graves with the personal belongings of their fallen kin. They developed more efficient weapons to improve hunting, but, surprisingly, tribal warfare appears to have been minimal.

Music played an important role in human culture, and the first known instrument was a bone flute found in France that dates to about 30,000 years ago. By about 23,000 years ago, bone sewing needles appeared in southwestern France, providing a sophisticated means of tailoring clothes made of animal hides. The earliest cloth did not appear until about 9,000 years ago. One of the most important developments was the trading of goods over long distances, especially of body ornaments, such as seashells used for making necklaces, which have been found at sites up to 100 miles inland from the ocean. People also made jewelry from stone and ivory beads, and from the teeth of dangerous animals such as bears and lions.

Cave paintings were a common form of human expression. Cavern walls in the French Pyrenees are covered with more than 200 hand prints, mostly with missing fingers, dated at about 26,000 years old. The fingers might have been destroyed by disease or infection or hacked off in a religious ritual. The late ice age people also made cave drawings of animals they pursued in the hunt (Fig. 1-12). Brazilian cave paintings suggest that cave art began in the Americas at about the same time it appeared in Europe and Africa.

THE NEOLITHIC REVOLUTION

Around 15,000 years ago, while hunting deer and wildebeest and gathering food along the North African coast, primitive peoples stumbled upon the rich Levant region bordering the eastern Mediterranean Sea. People also discovered an area known as the Fertile Crescent, stretching from the southeast coast of the Mediterranean to the Persian Gulf—the region presently occupied by Syria and Iraq. The discovery of abundant stands of wild wheat and barley growing in thickets on the uplands was among the most momentous events in human history.

The late Stone Age peoples gathered the wild plants and used primitive stone grinders to process the cereals. The stability of this food supply encouraged people to build permanent settlements. They devised a number of tools to harvest the crop and invented pottery in which to store and cook it. They might have herded gazelle rather than deplete them by overhunting, leading to a new system of animal husbandry. Wild dogs were tamed to manage chores, such as rounding up herds and warning of danger.

The Neolithic, or New Stone Age, which began at the end of the last ice age around 10,000 years ago, was the beginning of a food-producing revolution. Agriculture sprang up at about the same time in parts of the Old World and a few thousand years later in the New World, where one of the earliest archaeological records was that of the cultivation of maize (corn) in the Amazon region of South America around 3,000 years ago. Even in

Figure 1–13 Megalithic monuments scattered around Europe might have had an astronomical function.

Figure 1–14 A cliff house of the Anasazi Indians at Mesa Verde National Park, Colorado. Photo by C. H. Dane, courtesy of USGS

its earliest stages, agriculture was so productive it could support several times more people in a given area than could hunting and gathering.

The first Neolithic industry was the manufacture of pottery and plaster between 7000 and 6000 B.C. Plaster was probably invented as early as 14,000 years ago, long before pottery. Plaster artifacts discovered in the Near East include flooring material, containers, sculptures, and ornamental beads. The introduction of agriculture required more durable storage vessels for agricultural goods, resulting in the invention of ceramic pottery.

During the Neolithic, people built megalithic monuments (Fig. 1-13), such as Stonehenge in southern England, which are among the most dramatic remains of prehistoric culture around the world. Apparently, many of the hundreds of circles of tall monoliths scattered around Europe were used for astronomical purposes, such as the telling of the seasons. Others might have been erected for religious ceremonies. The oldest monuments are about 6,000 years old and are often composed of exotic rock hauled in from far away.

In the American Southwest stand the adobe dwellings of the Anasazi Indians (Fig. 1-14), who mysteriously disappeared during the middle 13th century A.D., possibly due to a prolonged period of drought. Other Native Americans left petroglyphs—images of animals and other figures carved or painted on cave walls. Originally, many of these carvings were thought to be simple pieces of cave art. However, some bear a definite relationship to the sun's path across the sky. One of the most striking examples is in the Cave of Life in the heart of the Petrified Forest in Arizona. On a stone wall there is a carving of an elaborate cross. When the rays of the setting sun strike the center of the cross, they mark the winter solstice, the shortest day of the year. Another cave, at Painted Rocks near Gila Bend, Arizona, has a similar cross carved on the cavern wall, possibly for the same reason. Their purpose remains a mystery, however. Perhaps they were used as calendars to determine the seasons of the year—an important tool for deciding when to plant and harvest crops to ensure the survival of the species.

2

THE POPULATION EXPLOSION

If a single day were to represent the Earth's entire history, then civilization and all its trappings began less than one second before midnight. In a mere 10,000 years following the last ice age, the number of humans increased exponentially, from about 5 million to over a thousand times that many today. Astronomically large numbers such as 5 billion are often difficult to grasp. Our planet is nearly 5 billion years old, so roughly one person is alive today for every year since the Earth's beginning. Another way to understand the immense human population is to imagine a line of people standing shoulder to shoulder, stretching 50 times around the world or five times the distance to the Moon.

THE BIRTH OF AGRICULTURE

For hundreds of thousands of years, humans were highly successful hunter-gatherers. The need to be constantly on the move kept the environment healthy and kept human populations from soaring beyond the carrying capacity of the land—that is, the maximum number of individuals a habitat can support. In the populations of hunter-gatherers, the growth rate—the difference between the birthrate and the death rate—approached zero.

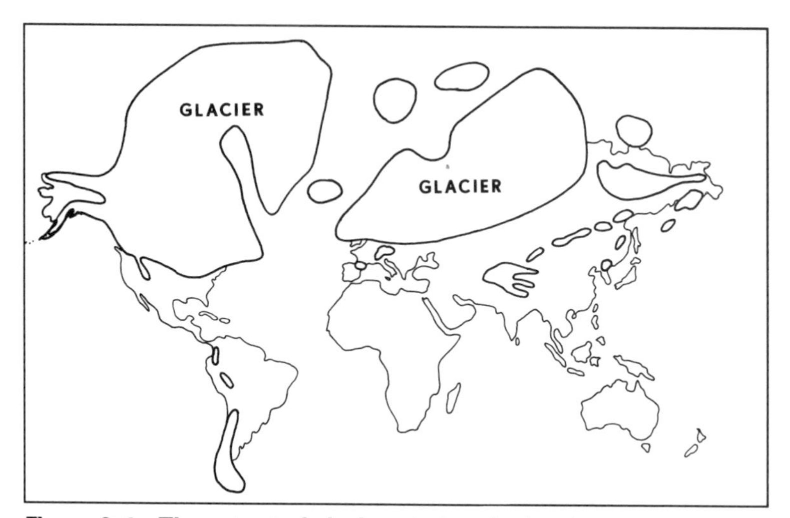

Figure 2–1 The extent of glaciers during the last ice age.

Rapid rises in population might have occurred during optimum conditions, but these might have been followed by catastrophic setbacks. During the coldest part of the last ice age, around 70,000 years ago (Fig. 2-1), humans were nearly an extinct species, until a population explosion brought on by extensive migration throughout the world set the stage for the emergence of fully modern humans.

Only out of a desperate need to feed their constantly growing numbers did primitive peoples reluctantly adopt the practice of agriculture. The dawn of agriculture at the beginning of the Neolithic period, about 10,000 years ago, was one of the greatest achievements in the history of the human race. However, this advance came at a heavy price. Although agriculture freed societies from the constant search for food, giving people more time for other aspects of life, it also made people territorial by allowing them to settle permanently in one place.

The introduction of agriculture encouraged a sedentary life-style, and permanent villages sprang up across Eurasia. Land ownership made people fight fiercely to protect their property. The land was cultivated and tended with care by the whole community so that it could be passed on to future generations. Agriculture both supported and encouraged population growth because it was labor-intensive, requiring large families to till and harvest the land. Unfortunately, increasing populations required intensification of food production, often with disastrous consequences to the land. In northern Syria, the community at Abu Hureyra was apparently abandoned about 5,000 B.C. because of the exhaustion of natural resources; this seems to have been a common pattern in early settlements (Fig. 2-2).

Figure 2–2 Ancient adobe dwellings of the Anasazi Indians at Pueblo Bonito in Chaco Canyon, New Mexico. They might have been forced out of the region because of a period of prolonged drought. Photo by George A. Grant, courtesy of National Park Service

Agriculture brought gross social inequalities, corruption, disease, and despotism. The freedoms of the simple hunting and gathering way of life gave way to a complex culture, and slavery appeared. Farm workers developed deformities in their legs, feet, and backs from carrying heavy loads and from the relentless hand-milling of grain. The health of the population also suffered as a result of a monotonous diet, gaining cheap calories at the cost of poor nutrition; hunter-gatherers on the other hand had always enjoyed a variety of foods.

Crowded conditions led to the spread of parasites and infectious diseases. The average height of early farmers fell several inches compared to hunter-gatherers. Average life expectancy dropped from 30 years to just 20 years, due in large part to the hard labor demanded by agriculture. Those who remained hunter-gatherers, had a comparatively leisurely life, spending considerably less time searching for food in the wild than farmers spent laboring in their fields.

Prior to the introduction of agriculture, mothers spaced their children far enough apart in age so they did not have to transport more than one baby during their nomadic existence. In contrast, farm women tended to have frequent pregnancies to produce more workers to till the land. The young were weaned early so that mothers could help work the fields as well. The shortened weaning period also increased the number of pregnancies, and women commonly had seven or more children in a lifetime.

A shortened life span brought about by the heavy burdens of agriculture required early and frequent pregnancies to maintain population growth, as well. Infant mortality was high, so women needed to maximize their number of babies. A high reproduction rate might have been crucial in the early days of civilization, when crop failures or disease frequently struck down entire populations. But rather than limit population growth during times of stress, people chose instead to attempt to increase food production to stave off starvation.

As populations increased, there was a need for improved farming techniques to increase food production; this led to the invention of the plow and the development of irrigation. Often these measures were inadequate, and overpopulation exhausted natural resources. People were thus forced to migrate to other regions, leaving behind a desolated landscape.

The progress of agriculture was not steady but was punctuated by fits and starts. In parts of northern Europe, the hunting and gathering life-style was so successful that the advent of agriculture was long delayed. Eventually, competition with agriculture disrupted the nomadic way of life. Farmers spread out across Europe, following the tracks of the hunter-gatherers, who themselves followed the retreating glaciers from the last ice age northward (Fig. 2-3).

About 6000 B.C., agriculture began to spread throughout Asia and Europe. The European continent at this time was largely forested, and huge tracts

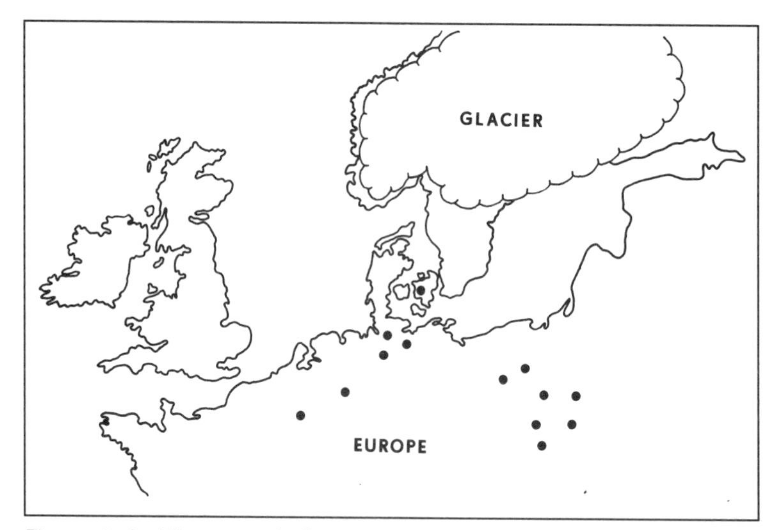

Figure 2–3 The spread of agriculture in northern Europe following the retreat of glacial ice, about 10,000 years ago.

Figure 2–4a Saguaro and other desert vegetation in the Sonora Desert, Arizona. Photo by W. T. Lee, courtesy of USGS

of land were cleared for cultivation. About 5,000 years ago, agriculture reached northern Europe and the British Isles, which had been settled during the ice age, when the English Channel and the North Sea basin were exposed above sea level as the ocean fell by as much as 400 feet.

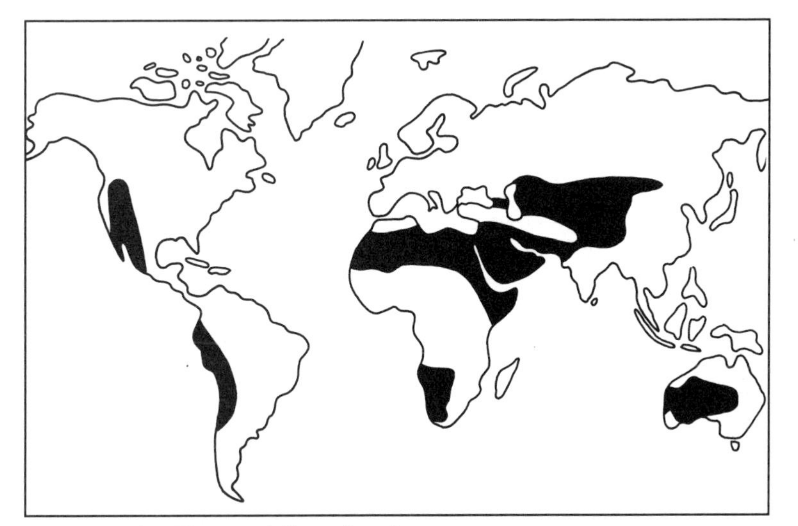

Figure 2–4b The world's major deserts.

About 4,000 years ago, the climate grew drier and the present deserts formed (Figs. 2-4a&b). On the arid plains of Mesopotamia, in southwest Asia, large irrigation projects required the hard labor of hundreds of thousands of people, and a system of centralized authority was devised to keep the population in line. In a mere thousand years, agriculture transformed a loose-knit egalitarian society based on equality into a strongly ruled authoritarian society, equipped with masters and slaves.

People used fire to bake ceramic pottery and forge bronze tools and weapons. Bronze metallurgy spread rapidly through Europe, due in part to large-scale population movements. The Greeks mined the island of Cyprus extensively for the copper and tin used to make bronze, as indicated by mining tools dating prior to 2500 B.C. found in the underground mine workings. The Bronze Age gave way to the Iron Age about 1000 B.C., when the disruption of the tin trade forced the Greeks to search for a suitable bronze substitute. All this time, the use of fire was still rudimentary—in fact, it remained so until the introduction of the steam engine in the late 1700s. The steam engine ushered in the industrial age, and for the first time people freed their muscles from the drudgery of hard labor. But this was a costly advance.

THE INDUSTRIAL AGE

Europe's Industrial Revolution was a major breakthrough in human progress and a powerful stimulus for rapid population growth (Fig. 2-5). The vicious cycle of overpopulation followed by famine and disease was finally broken. During the hundred years between 1750 and 1850, the world's population growth accelerated at an unprecedented 0.5 percent per year. But as industry expanded, it also brought horrible evils, like low wages and terrible factory working conditions. Yet overall, the human condition generally improved with industrialization and the innovations and institutions it fostered.

Prior to the industrial era, the small fires of civilization had virtually no effect on the environment. However, as populations continued growing as a direct result of industrialization, the need for fuel increased and Europe's forests were in danger of being destroyed for firewood—until the timely discovery of coal. Actually, the existence of coal had been known for quite some time. Early peoples probably discovered it when lightning ignited coal outcrops, and for centuries Native Americans had used coal for their cooking fires.

In Europe, coal fueled the engines of the early industrial age. It stoked the furnaces of the factories and foundries, which were often located near the coal mines to minimize transportation. Work in the mines was often backbreaking and dangerous, and wages were poor. When industrialization

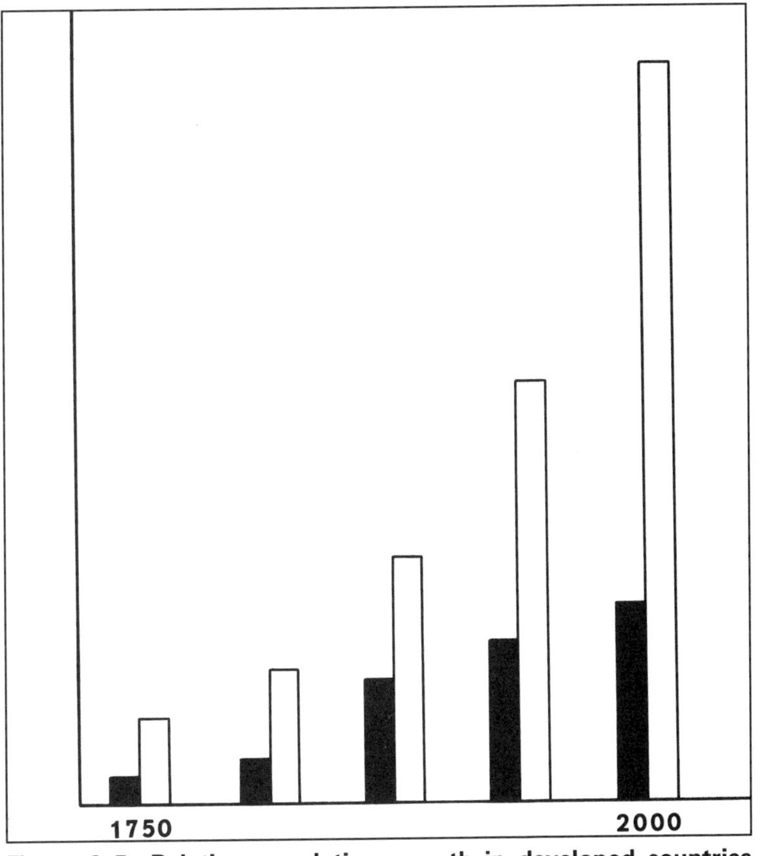

Figure 2–5 Relative population growth in developed countries (black bar) and undeveloped countries (white bar).

reached America, families settled in company-owned mining towns, where the prices for rent and supplies were often higher than the miners' wages, causing many to work themselves into debt.

By the middle of the 18th century, the Industrial Revolution had spread throughout Britain and Europe. However, it did not make its debut in the United States for almost another century, because the U.S. economy was mostly agrarian. In the South, cotton was king and slavery its realm. Even at the beginning of the 20th century, half of all Americans still lived and worked on farms. By comparison, Europe's populations were becoming more urban than rural. The lure of the big cities and the promise of better-paying jobs prompted a wave of migration from farm to factory occupations. New inventions proliferated; they included steam locomotives and steamships, which carried goods throughout the world to feed a hungry industrial giant.

Figure 2–6 Littered beach on Clear Lake near Natchitoches, Louisiana. Photo by M. J. Hough, courtesy of USDA–Soil Conservation Service

Great industries gave rise to huge industrial cities, where smoke belched from a profusion of chimneys. Although the population generally benefited from the economic prosperity of industrialization, people also suffered in many ways. There were serious health hazards: Smoke was so heavy that people died in unusually large numbers from respiratory ailments. Ash and soot were pervasive, blackening buildings, trees, and other objects. Smoke belching from factories stung the eyes, and the sulfurous stench of burning coal constantly hung in the air. Some days the smoke was so thick it blocked out the sun, turning day into dusk.

The industrial age brought prosperity and rapid population growth, which in turn required additional industrialization. With more mouths to feed, more forests were cleared to make room for additional agriculture. Rapid-paced industrialization brought greater economic security, but at the cost of increasing amounts of pollution (Fig. 2-6).

POPULATION GROWTH

Two million years ago, the food-gathering peoples of Africa numbered perhaps 100,000. When agriculture was introduced shortly after the last ice age ended about 10,000 years ago, 5 to 10 million people occupied the planet. During the first Egyptian dynasty, about 5,000 years ago, the population rose to 100 million. At the height of the Roman Empire about 2,000 years ago, the world's population was more than 250 million—close to the present population of the United States. By the beginning of the Industrial Revolution in 1750, the population had tripled from Roman times. The rapid population growth was mainly a result of falling death rates caused by a drop in infant mortality and an increase in life expectancy.

The human population reached its first billion mark around 1800, and 130 years later, in 1930, it had doubled to 2 billion. In just 45 years, by 1975, it doubled again to 4 billion, cutting the doubling time by two-thirds. The 5 billion mark was reached in 1987, and another billion is expected by 1997. Even these figures are only crude estimates based on census counts. Not all countries take a census of their people, and those that do inevitably undercount populations. Furthermore, the migrations of large numbers of people from war-torn or impoverished regions make accurate census-taking impossible. Therefore, the actual number of people in the world is probably higher than indicated.

The rapid gain in life expectancy in the developing countries since World War II has been one of the main causes of the explosive population growth. Their populations are likely to triple in the next century, and more than half their people will live in urban areas. At an average annual growth rate of about 1.7 percent, the global human population could reach 14 billion or more by the middle of the next century, with a doubling rate of 40 to 50 years. Moreover, the doubling rate has decreased steadily over this century, with some regions experiencing doubling rates of less than 20 years.

If the population continued doubling every generation or so, in 500 years one person would occupy every square meter (about 10 square feet) of the total land surface of the Earth. In about a thousand years, humans would outweigh the planet. Obviously, this is a ridiculous notion, for as with bacteria grown in a petri dish, humans would either consume all the nutrients or suffocate in their own waste products long before that happens.

Since 1930, human numbers have grown from 2 billion to over 5 billion, increasing faster than in the entire preceding span of human history, with as many people alive today as have ever lived and died. Furthermore, the developing countries, which have the highest populations, are growing more than twice as fast as the developed nations. The high population growth in the developed nations was due largely to the baby boom of the 1950s and 1960s, following World War II. The United States has added another 100 million people to its population since 1948. Furthermore, lifeexpectancy has increased and infant mortality has decreased in the developing countries as well as in the developed world.

TABLE 2–1 WORLD POPULATION AT 1.7 PERCENT ANNUAL GROWTH

Date	Population in Billions	Date	Population in Billions
1987	5.00	2019	8.58
1988	5.09	2020	8.72
1989	5.17	2021	8.87
1990	5.26	2022	9.02
1991	5.35	2023	9.17
1992	5.44	2024	9.33
1993	5.53	2025	9.49
1994	5.63	2026	9.65
1995	5.72	2027	9.81
1996	5.82	2028	9.98
1997	5.92	2029	10.15
1998	6.02	2030	10.32
1999	6.12	2031	10.49
2000	6.23	2032	10.68
2001	6.33	2033	10.86
2002	6.44	2034	11.04
2003	6.55	2035	11.23
2004	6.66	2036	11.42
2005	6.77	2037	11.61
2006	6.89	2038	11.81
2007	7.01	2039	12.01
2008	7.12	2040	12.22
2009	7.24	2041	12.43
2010	7.37	2042	12.64
2011	7.49	2043	12.85
2012	7.62	2044	13.07
2013	7.75	2045	13.29
2014	7.88	2046	13.52
2015	8.02	2047	13.75
2016	8.15	2048	13.98
2017	8.29	2049	14.22
2018	8.43	2050	14.46

The growth in human population reached a climax in the third quarter of this century and now appears to be abating somewhat. However, population growth has a large built-in momentum—that is, today's offspring are going to produce children of their own, inevitably causing another doubling of the population. This situation virtually assures major increases in population size, especially in countries that contain a large majority of the world's people. Therefore, barring a natural disaster or government coercion, human population growth is unlikely to abate, and another doubling of human numbers seems inevitable. The United Nations conference on population and development held in Cairo, Egypt in September 1994 desired to stabilize the number of people at 7.2 billion.

Many demographers who study human populations believe the world is already at or has exceeded its carrying capacity. A population exceeds carrying capacity when it cannot be maintained without rapidly depleting nonrenewable resources (Fig. 2-7) and degrading the environment. By that definition, most countries are therefore already vastly overpopulated. Moreover, carrying capacity is not a definable number such as 5 or 10 billion people. The Earth could support twice as many vegetarians on bicycles as meat eaters in automobiles without serious damage to the

Figure 2–7 Oil well drilling on Alaska's North Slope, Barrow district, Alaska.
Photo by J. C. Reed, courtesy of US Navy and USGS

environment. But at the present level of environmental degradation, even 5 billion people might surpass the Earth's carrying capacity. The human race seems to be conducting a dangerous experiment to see how many people can be crammed onto the planet before the entire biological system collapses.

At the present rate of growth, it would be difficult to feed, clothe, shelter, and employ many additional people at more than a subsistence level of life. Meanwhile, the population growth of many developed nations has stabilized, and misguided governments mostly in Europe are demanding higher birth rates to maintain economic growth. The problem becomes even more exacerbated as the population ages, putting a greater burden on workers to support the growing numbers of nonproductive elderly who are living longer and have higher medical expenses. By the middle of the next century, the number of people 65 years or older could expand to at least 2.5 billion, or about one-fifth of the world's projected population. With death rates continuing to decrease in the developing countries, more than 90 percent of the population can expect to live past the age of 65.

If the population continues growing at its astounding rate, the number of people living in the world today could more than double by the year 2050. Over 95 percent of the increase would occur in the undeveloped countries, particularly in Africa, whose people would constitute over a quarter of the human race. Between 1950 and 1985, the net addition of humans in the undeveloped countries was about 2 billion, a number equal to the entire world population in 1930 and over twice the figure for the total

TABLE 2–2 GLOBAL AGE DISTRIBUTION BY PERCENT

	Age in Years				
Area	0 to 4	5 to 14	15 to 64	65	Fertility Rate*
Developed countries	7.6	15.5	65.6	11.3	2.1
Japan	7.3	16.1	67.7	8.9	1.7
England	7.9	15.0	66.3	10.7	1.8
Hungary	8.0	13.7	64.9	15.9	1.9
Developing countries	13.6	25.5	57.0	4.0	4.2
Korea	10.6	22.7	62.2	4.0	3.0
Colombia	14.0	25.4	57.1	3.5	3.7
Bangladesh	17.9	24.9	54.6	2.6	6.4
Kenya	22.4	28.6	46.1	2.9	8.0

*Number of live births per woman

population of the developed countries at mid-century. By the year 2000, if predictions hold true, half the people in the undeveloped countries will be under the age of 15, requiring nearly a billion new jobs when they reach maturity and begin raising families of their own. Twenty cities, mostly in the undeveloped countries, will have populations exceeding 10 million people. Many cities could become sprawling slums, with few services and much disease, pollution, crime, unemployment, and political unrest.

Mexico City, the world's largest metropolis, could attain a population of over 30 million by the year 2000. At the same time, Bangladesh could increase its population by 60 percent, with 160 million people squeezed

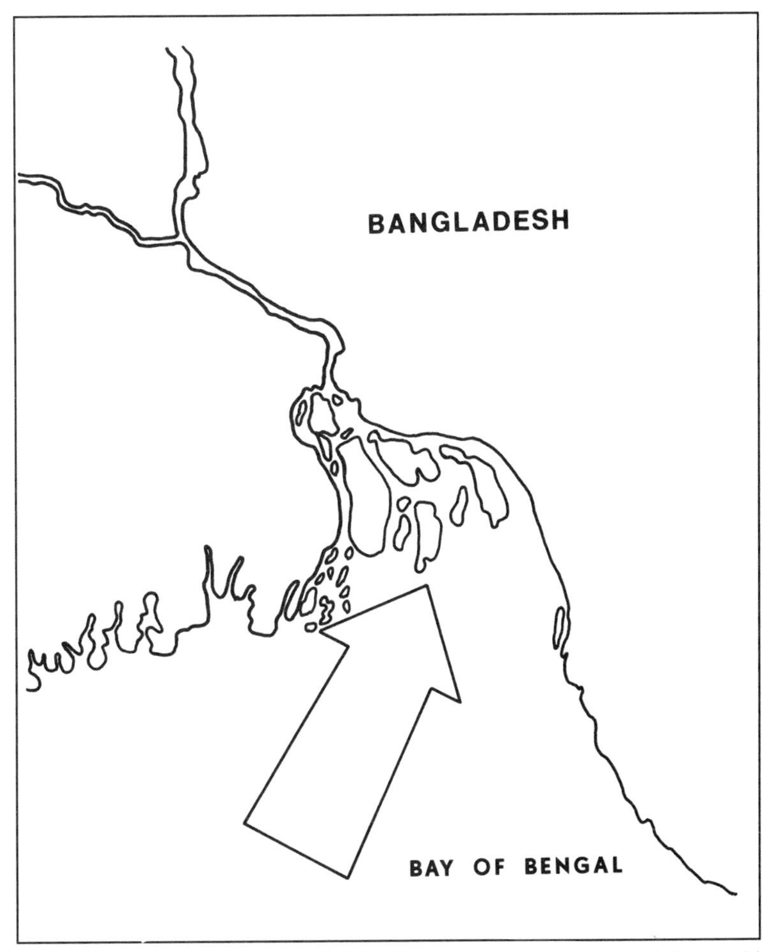

Figure 2–8 Path taken by the May 24, 1985, Bay of Bengal/ Bangladesh typhoon that killed upwards of 100,000 people.

into an area about the size of Wisconsin. The tiny island of Macau, located off the coast of China west of Hong Kong, is the most densely populated place on Earth. Some 350,000 people are jammed onto only 6 square miles, or about 60,000 people per square mile. If the population were spread evenly throughout the island, one person would occupy the space of a quarter of a tennis court.

The most densely populated regions are islands and low-lying river deltas like Bangladesh, which has nearly 2,000 people per square mile in an area that is extremely vulnerable to tropical storms (Fig. 2-8). High population density usually indicates good climatic and growing conditions, with no deserts, mountains, or other impediments to human habitation. The countries that are the most sparsely populated often have poor climates or uninhabitable geographies. About a third of the world's landmass is composed of uninhabited wilderness areas. However, only half of these regions are self-protected by virtue of their forbidding nature (Fig. 2-9). The rest of the wilderness is in danger of disappearing as a result of the encroachment of humans.

Figure 2–9 Alluvial fans off the Diamond Mountains, Nevada, one of the most inhospitable places in the world. Photo by J. R. Balsley, courtesy of USGS

OVERPOPULATION

Until recently, the effects of the population explosion have been largely excluded from the debate on the deteriorating condition of the Earth. Human populations are growing so explosively and modifying the environment so extensively that the impact is global and unprecedented. During the past few decades, humans have brought about major changes to the Earth, comparable in magnitude to some of the worst calamities wrought by nature over geologic time, including the extinction of species (Fig. 2-10). The damage to the planet continues to escalate as long as burgeoning human populations grow out of control. To keep up with basic human requirements, a five- to tenfold increase in world economic activity over the next half century would be required—a situation the biosphere cannot possibly tolerate without irreversible damage.

Despite prosperity in the world as a whole, famine persists in many places. While the world's population increases, per capita food output is

Figure 2–10 Geologists unearthing large fossil bones, possible evidence of a mass extinction, near Littleton, Colorado. Photo by J. R. Stacy, courtesy of USGS

Figure 2–11 Flooded farmsteads on the left bank of the Bighorn River near Hardin, Montana on May 19, 1978. Photo by C. Parrett, courtesy of USGS

declining. The relationship between population density and food supply is well demonstrated in the natural world, where animal populations are limited by the amount of available food. However, this relationship does not always hold for humans. People can and do survive on much less than the optimum amount of food, although they do not live very long at this level of bare subsistence.

According to the 19th-century English economist Thomas Malthus, the lowest level of subsistence is a food supply just sufficient to sustain life obtained by the maximum work effort the population can exert. Malthus also believed that human populations are limited by the food supply because they grow geometrically (by increments of 2, 4, 8, 16, 32, and so on), while food production only increases arithmetically (2, 4, 6, 8, 10, and so on). Humans tend to increase their numbers beyond the carrying capacity of the land until famine, war, or disease wipes out the excess.

Unless food is in extremely short supply, most adults do not die immediately from an inadequate diet. Eventually, however, vitality, health, and ability to work suffer. In populations with meager diets, fertility also might be depressed, or pregnancy and nursing might cause a too-severe energy drain on the mother. Furthermore, damage to the intestinal tract caused by parasites and infection causes the body to utilize food less efficiently, thereby requiring a higher intake to stay alive.

Because of their rapid body growth, most children do not survive their first year of severe malnutrition. Up to half the children of Africa below the age of five have abnormally low body weights. Young children who survive a famine often suffer irreversible damage—disease, stunted growth, blindness, and mental illness. What might emerge from a famine is a new generation of young survivors, who are severely handicapped and weakened to the point where they cannot care for themselves and thereby become an additional burden on society.

In developing countries, which have the highest birthrates—averaging about 5.5 children per mother—economic growth has been stifled because

Figure 2–12 A road adjacent to an unprotected cotton field is buried during a dust storm near Floydada, Texas on January 25, 1965. Photo by G. E. Black, courtesy of USDA–Soil Conservation Service

any economic gains are quickly eroded by the increasing number of mouths to feed. In Kenya, which has the world's highest birthrate, the average mother used to have eight babies, half of whom did not survive. However, with improved health care she now has eight living children. Furthermore, better health is leading to more adolescent sexual promiscuity and a flood of unwanted pregnancies in most countries. Thus, the developing nations, in Asia, Africa, and South America are in a desperate race to keep food supplies growing at the same rate as the population, often with disastrous consequences for their land.

During favorable climatic periods, populations tend to grow well beyond the limits imposed by unfavorable climates, when harvests are poor (Fig. 2-11). And few developing countries can produce a surplus of food in good years to tide them over during lean years. As a result, they are extremely vulnerable to fluctuations in the climate. When food prices rise due to crop failures, poor families must forego other necessities to obtain food, further lowering their already poor standards of living. Unless constraints are placed on the burgeoning human population, more misery is likely to occur, especially among poor nations. Due to the loss of topsoil, many developing countries have already exceeded the carrying capacity of their land and cannot survive without outside aid.

As world populations continue growing geometrically on a planet whose resources are dwindling rapidly, the vast majority of people are forced to live on a bare subsistence level. As a hungry world crowds onto worn-out soils, man-made deserts continue to encroach on once-fertile lands (Fig. 2-12).

3

THE BALANCE OF NATURE

Many aspects of life on Earth are governed by cycles, and any interference with these cycles can spell catastrophe. The continuous evaporation of seawater and its precipitation on the continents is one of nature's most important cycles, providing water for life on the Earth's surface. The circulation of carbon maintains the balance between incoming and outgoing thermal energy, determining the temperature of the planet. In fact, without the greenhouse effect, which traps heat in the atmosphere, nothing could live. The recycling of nitrogen in the biosphere is also fundamental for the support of living beings on this planet.

THE GAIA HYPOTHESIS

The Earth not only provides life with all the essentials it needs to survive, but life also appears to have made its own changes in order to maintain itself at optimal levels. The Gaia hypothesis, named for the Greek goddess of the Earth, suggests that life, to some extent, controls its own environment to optimize living conditions; it portrays the planet as a single huge living organism that creates a favorable environment for itself. The interaction

between the living and nonliving thus creates a self-regulating system that keeps itself in a constant state of equilibrium.

Life defined in physical terms is a huge, intricate molecular machine that seems to overcome, at least for a short while, the second law of thermodynamics, which essentially states that every form of order eventually dissolves into chaos. Life manages to go against the flow of a steadily decaying universe. But the uphill struggle comes at the expense of a great deal of energy supplied by the sun. This energy is manifested by the presence of large amounts of oxygen in the atmosphere, since without life, chemical reactions would have run downhill and all oxygen would have long ago been bound to other elements.

Originally, the atmosphere contained 25 percent carbon dioxide, about the same amount of oxygen today. Because the sun's output was about a third less than it is now, the high levels of carbon dioxide helped to maintain the Earth's temperature. Without this stabilizing gas, the planet would have completely frozen over, and because ice is such a good reflector of sunlight the Earth would have remained an icy orb.

When green plants evolved, they gradually replaced carbon dioxide with oxygen through photosynthesis, which manufactures organic compounds and produces oxygen as a by-product. This was fortunate, because at the same time the sun was becoming progressively hotter, and large amounts of atmospheric carbon dioxide were no longer needed. If carbon dioxide had not been removed from the atmosphere by the biosphere, the Earth would have suffered the same fate as Venus, whose high surface temperatures evaporated its oceans eons ago. Moreover, if the Earth had begun with the atmosphere it has today, it would have been as cold as Mars. Either way, life could not have survived.

At first, simple organisms lived in an anaerobic (lacking oxygen) environment, in which oxygen was poisonous to life. When photosynthesis first evolved, as early as 3.5 billion years ago, all oxygen that was produced bonded to chemical elements and was permanently locked up in the Earth's crust. About 2 billion years ago, these oxygen sinks held all the oxygen they could contain, and the gas began slowly to build up in the ocean and the atmosphere. As oxygen production reached higher levels, complex organisms began to evolve. When the level was near where it is today, the ozone screen made it possible for plants and animals to conquer the land.

Life appears to maintain oxygen and carbon dioxide in a perfect balance, and too much of one in relation to the other could have disastrous consequences. Life forms use the atmosphere both as a source of raw materials, such as oxygen and nitrogen, and as a repository for waste products, such as carbon dioxide, an important greenhouse gas. In this manner, life is directly linked to the greenhouse effect, and living organisms can regulate the climate to their benefit. Thus, without life the Earth's climate would be wildly out of control.

THE PRECARIOUS BALANCE

A fortunate set of circumstances has held global temperatures to within the range of the freezing and boiling points of water. The Earth's distance from the sun has a major effect on the planet's temperature range, as a distance difference of only 10 percent could spell the difference between life or death. Even minor changes in orbital variations can initiate the onset of ice ages (Fig. 3-1).

The climate is most significantly affected by the greenhouse effect, which traps solar energy that would otherwise escape into space (Fig. 3-2). If Mars had Venus's heavy carbon dioxide atmosphere it would be hotter than Earth despite being farther from the sun, because a strong greenhouse effect would retain what little heat Mars receives from the sun—heat normally lost to space. On the other hand, if Venus, the closer planet to the sun, had Mars' thin carbon dioxide atmosphere, it would be colder than Earth.

To a great extent, life began because of the greenhouse effect. Large quantities of greenhouse gases in the early atmosphere maintained temperatures within tolerable, life-sustaining limits, even though the sun's heat output was lower than it is today. Fluctuations in the carbon dioxide content of the atmosphere have resulted in major changes in the world's climate. During the ice ages, when the carbon cycle removed too much carbon dioxide from the atmosphere, temperatures plummeted and great ice sheets flowed across the land. When excessive volcanic

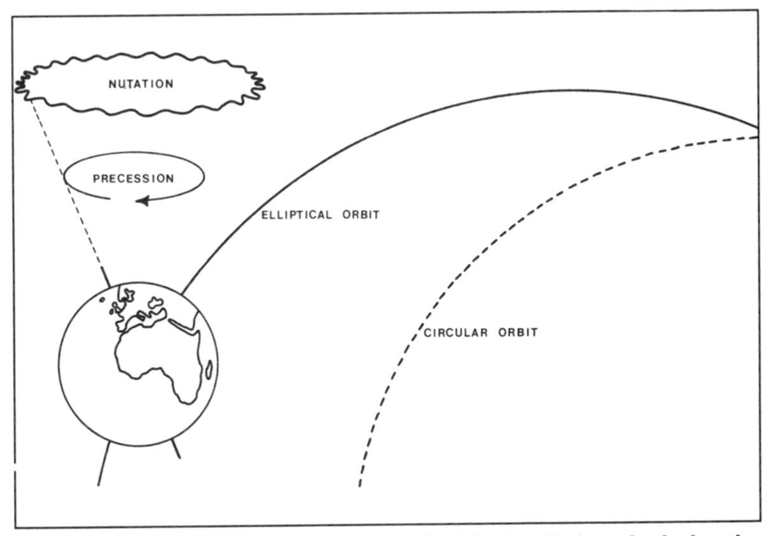

Figure 3–1 The Milankovich model of orbital variations includes the 100,000-year orbital cycle, the 41,000-year nutation cycle, and the 22,000-year precession cycle.

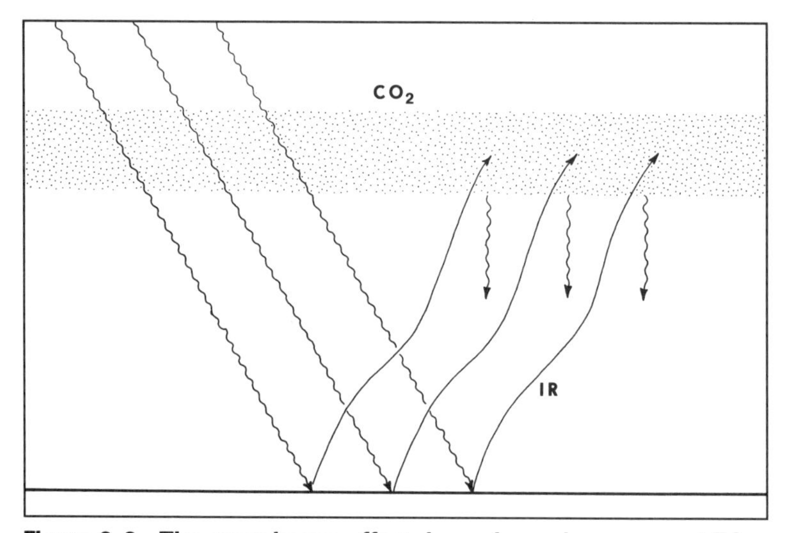

Figure 3–2 The greenhouse effect. Incoming solar energy striking the surface is converted to infrared radiation (IR) that is trapped by atmospheric greenhouse gases, including CO_2.

activity added too much carbon dioxide to the atmosphere, temperatures soared and the Earth became a hothouse. Only when carbon dioxide levels remain fairly constant does the climate maximize benefits for all living things.

The ecosphere, which integrates life with other Earth processes, provides living beings with all the essentials they need to survive. Life also might have made major changes of its own to maintain optimum living conditions—as suggested in the Gaia hypothesis. The biosphere, the portion of the Earth in which life exists, appears to be capable of controlling its environment by regulating the climate to some extent, similar to the way the human body regulates its temperature to optimize metabolic efficiency. For example, a certain species of plankton releases a sulfur compound into the atmosphere that aids in the formation of clouds. If the Earth warms, plankton growth is invigorated, releasing more cloud-forming sulfur compounds to cool the planet and stabilize temperatures.

Life can be considered a major "geologic" force that has extensively changed the Earth. Although the species most frequently encountered on the surface would seem to be the most influential in shaping the planet, the greatest influence actually comes from unseen microbes, which make up about 90 percent of the biomass—the total weight of all living matter. These are structurally simple creatures that are biochemically diverse, highly adaptive, and absolutely essential for maintaining living conditions on Earth.

Single-celled photosynthetic organisms that thrive in the sunlit zone of the ocean generate about 80 percent of atmospheric oxygen. Microorganisms like bacteria play a critical role by breaking down the remains of plants and animals to recycle nutrients in the biosphere. Land plants depend on bacteria in their root systems for nitrogen fixation. Bacteria live symbiotically in the digestive tracts of animals (including humans) and aid in the digestion of food. Simple organisms also comprise the bottom of the food chain, upon which all life ultimately depends for its survival.

Photosynthetic organisms store energy by combining carbon from atmospheric carbon dioxide with hydrogen from water to form carbohydrates. Thick coal deposits (Fig. 3-3) are essentially buried solar energy, because they originated as lush vegetative matter in ancient swamps. Vast subterranean reservoirs of petroleum are basically cooked hydrocarbon molecules from once-living microorganisms. These fossil fuels have been accumulating over eons. When they are burned in factories and automobiles, the equation reverses, and carbon is recombined with oxygen (Fig. 3-4), releasing carbon dioxide back into the atmosphere.

Humans are interfering with the carbon cycle by spewing massive quantities of carbon dioxide into the atmosphere from industrialization and habitat destruction including deforestation and loss of wetlands. In this manner, people are fast becoming the single most destructive force on the face of the planet, confounding nature's efforts to maintain balance.

Figure 3–3 A thick coal bed, Wainwright district, Alaska. Photo by R. M. Chapman, courtesy of USGS

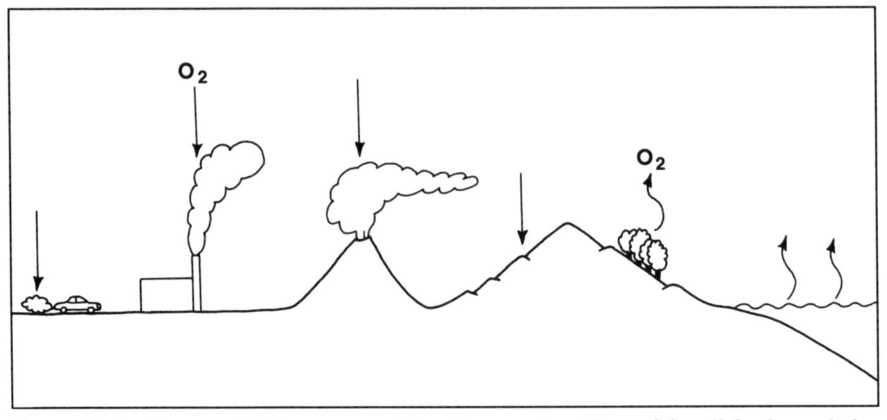

Figure 3–4 Oxygen (O_2) consumed by the combustion of fossil fuels and the oxidation of Earth materials is balanced by plant respiration on land and sea.

THE HEAT BUDGET

The atmosphere plays a critical role in sustaining life by maintaining the balance of incoming solar radiation and outgoing infrared radiation. The Earth intercepts about one-billionth of the sun's rays. Only about half of this solar energy reaches the surface, where 90 percent works to evaporate water, creating weather patterns. The Earth must reradiate back into space

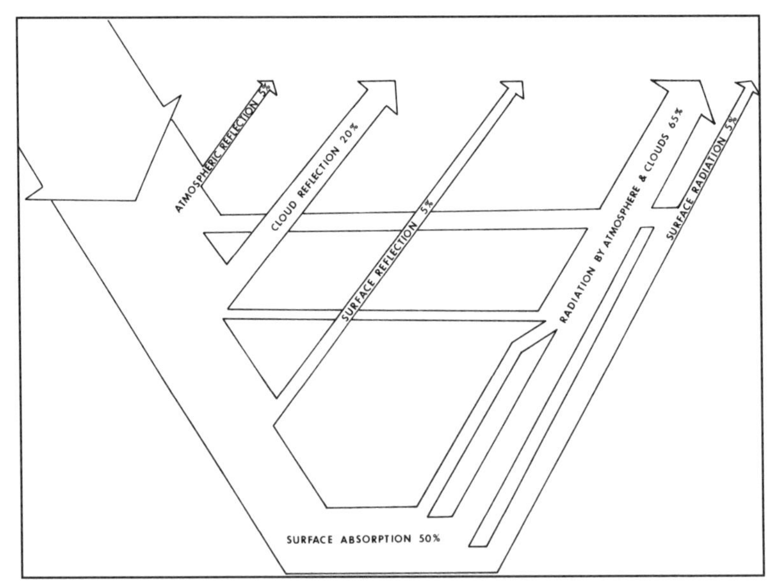

Figure 3–5 The Earth's heat budget.

the same amount of energy it receives from the sun; otherwise temperatures would become exceedingly hot. But if the Earth emits too much infrared energy, temperatures would turn unbearably cold. This delicate balancing act is known as the Earth's energy or heat budget (Fig. 3-5), which is responsible for maintaining global temperatures within the narrow confines that make life possible.

When sunlight strikes the Earth's surface, it is transformed into infrared energy, which is absorbed by the atmosphere, and then emitted to space. The angle at which sunlight strikes the surface determines the amount of solar energy being absorbed or reflected. In the tropics along the equator, the sun's rays strike the Earth from directly overhead, and more solar radiation is absorbed on the surface than is reflected into space. In the polar regions, the sun's rays strike the Earth at a low angle, and more solar radiation is reflected into space than is absorbed on the surface. If not for the distribution of heat by the atmosphere and the oceans, the tropics would swelter in heat and the higher latitudes would shiver in cold, to such a degree than no place on Earth could be inhabited

The heat budget is also responsible for generating the weather. Warm air rises at the equator in narrow columns and travels aloft toward the poles. In the polar regions, the air liberates heat, cools, sinks, and returns to the equator, where it warms again in a continuous cycle. Currents in the ocean

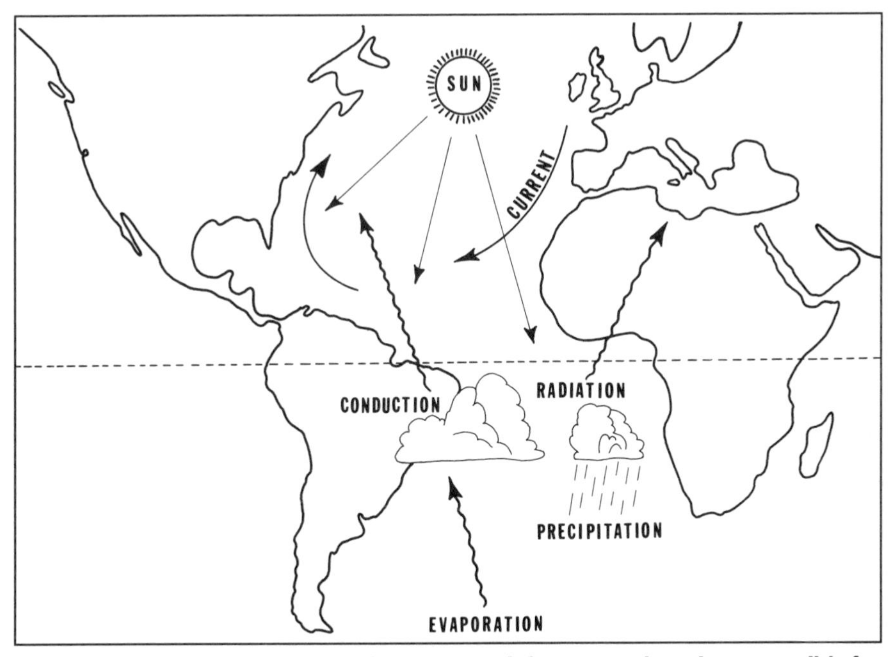

Figure 3–6 Heat flow between the ocean and the atmosphere is responsible for distributing the ocean's heat around the world.

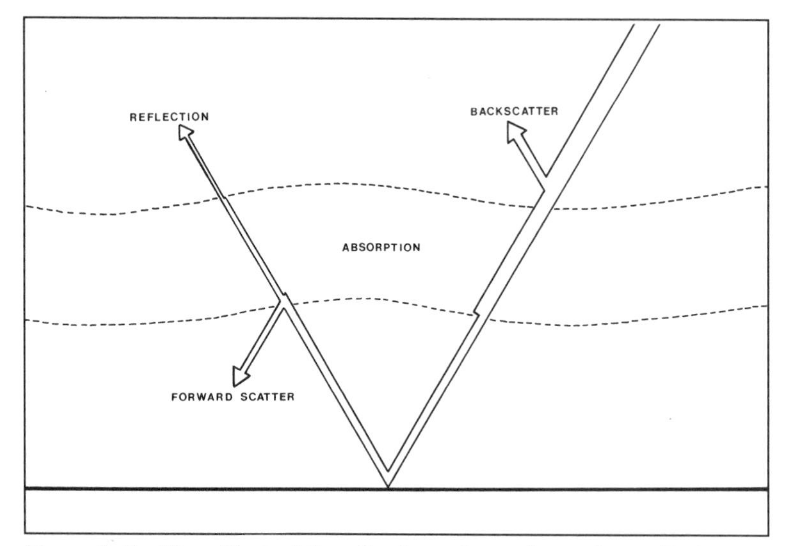

Figure 3–7 The effect of the albedo on incoming solar radiation.

TABLE 3–1 ALBEDO OF VARIOUS SURFACES

Surface	Percent Reflected
Clouds, stratus,	
< 500 feet thick	25–63
500–1,000 feet thick	45–75
1,000–2,000 feet thick	59–84
Average all types and thicknesses	50–55
Snow, fresh-fallen	80–90
Snow, old	45–70
White sand	30–60
Light soil (or desert)	25–30
Concrete	17–27
Plowed field, moist	14–17
Crops, green	5–25
Meadows, green	5–10
Forests, green	5–10
Dark soil	5–15
Road, blacktop	5–10
Water, depending upon sun angle	5–60

act in a similar manner, only more slowly, taking much longer to complete the journey. The middle latitudes, or temperate zones, become battlegrounds between warm, moist tropical air and cold, dry polar air. When these air masses clash, they create storms.

The oceans play a vital role in distributing solar energy. Solar radiation heats seawater, and thermal energy is transported by ocean currents, lost by conduction, radiation, and evaporation, and regained by precipitation. Heat flow between the oceans and the atmosphere is responsible for cloud formation. A tremendous amount of thermal energy is used to evaporate seawater into water vapor. When clouds move to other parts of the world, they liberate energy by precipitation, which circulates the ocean's heat around the world (Fig. 3-6).

The heat budget mostly depends on the albedo effect, which is an object's ability to reflect sunlight (Fig. 3-7). Some things reflect solar energy better than others, mainly due to their color. Light-colored objects, like clouds, snow fields, or deserts, reflect more solar energy than they absorb. Dark-colored objects, like oceans or forests, absorb more solar energy than they reflect. Most of the solar energy impinging on the ocean evaporates seawater, and this energy is lost to space when water vapor condenses into rain.

Figure 3–8 The Earth Radiation Budget Experiment (ERBE) satellite measures the Earth's albedo to anticipate climate trends that affect agriculture, energy, natural resources, transportation, and construction. Courtesy of NASA

One-third of the solar energy is reflected back into space before it has a chance to heat the Earth. Most of this lost energy reflects off clouds. Data taken from the Earth Radiation Budget Experiment satellite (Fig. 3-8) indicates that, on the whole, clouds exert a net cooling influence on the planet, and the effect is much stronger at mid-latitudes than in the tropics. High cirrus clouds retain the Earth's heat, whereas low stratus clouds block out the sun and cool the surface.

Only about half the total solar energy that impinges on the planet reaches the Earth's surface to heat the ocean and the land. Eventually, all sunlight that strikes the surface converts into infrared energy and radiates upward. If it were not for the greenhouse effect, which prevents all infrared energy from radiating into space, the entire Earth would be covered by a permanent sheet of ice.

THE WATER CYCLE

Our planet is the only body in the solar system that is known to possess water in all its states—solid, liquid, and gaseous. Three percent of the

Figure 3–9 Taylor Glacier region, Victoria Land, Antarctica. Photo by W. B. Hamilton, courtesy of USGS

Earth's water is fresh, enough to fill the mile-deep Mediterranean basin 10 times over. About three-quarters of the fresh water is locked up in glacial ice, 90 percent of which lies atop Antarctica (Fig. 3-9). The remaining water, less than 1 percent of the Earth's total, is atmospheric water vapor, running water in rivers, standing water in lakes, groundwater, soil moisture, and water in plant and animal tissues. About 15 percent of the moisture in the atmosphere originates from the land.

At its present temperature, the atmosphere can hold only about 0.5 percent of the Earth's water at any one time. However, increased temperatures induced by global warming could increase atmospheric water vapor, which also happens to be the most effective greenhouse gas. However, the increased cloud cover produced by the additional water vapor would probably balance out the greenhouse effect.

The oceans cover about 70 percent of the planet's surface to an average depth of over 2 miles. The total amount of seawater is about 300 billion cubic miles. Every day, a trillion tons of water rains down on the planet, but most falls directly into the sea. Water moves from the ocean, over the land, and back to the sea in one of nature's most important cycles, known as the hydrologic or water cycle (Fig. 3-10). Without the flow of water on the Earth, life as we know it could not exist.

The water travels from the ocean to the atmosphere, across the land, and back to the sea in about 10 days, on average. The journey takes only a few hours in the tropical coastal areas and as long as 10,000 years in the polar

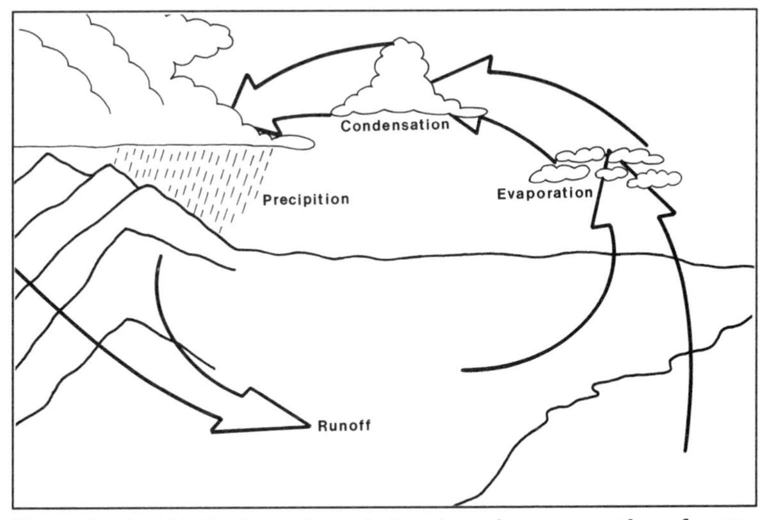

Figure 3–10 The hydrologic cycle involves the evaporation of water from the ocean and the land, the condensation into clouds, the precipitation on the land, and the return of runoff to the sea.

Figure 3–11 An iceberg in Glacier Bay, Alaska. Photo by G. K. Gilbert, courtesy of USGS

regions. Snow falling in the arctic regions builds glaciers that eventually either melt or plunge into the ocean as icebergs (Fig. 3-11). The quickest route water takes to the ocean is by runoff in streams and rivers. This is the most essential part of the water cycle. Rivers provide waterways for commerce and water for irrigation, hydroelectric power, municipal water supplies, and recreation.

The average annual rainfall over the land is roughly 25 inches. Some areas receive more rainfall than others: The tropical rain forests receive 200 to 400 inches per year, while deserts generally receive less than 10 inches per year. The amount of precipitation falling on the land is about 25,000 cubic miles annually, of which some 10,000 cubic miles is surplus water that is lost by floods, held by soils, or contained by wetlands. About a third of the total water the land receives is base flow, or the stable runoff of all the world's streams and rivers. The rest is groundwater flow. Some 15,000 cubic miles of water evaporates from lakes, rivers, aquifers, soils, and plants. Trees and other vegetation lose much water by transpiration, which is the evaporation of water from leaves and other plant parts.

A large amount of water the continents receive is lost by floods, which are naturally recurring events that are important for the distribution of soils over the land. During a flood, a river might change its course many times as it meanders along its journey to the sea, thus laying out a new floodplain.

Figure 3–12 Floodwaters of the Trinity River in April 1957 spread over bottomlands near Crockett, Houston County, Texas. Photo by I. D. Yost, courtesy of U.S. Army Corps of Engineers and USGS

The floodplains provide level ground and fertile soil and attract commerce. However, rapid development of these areas without consideration of the flood potential often leads to disaster (Fig. 3-12).

Since the 1930s the United States has spent some $10 billion on flood protection projects, most of which are levees that keep rivers in their channels and reservoirs that even out the flow rates of rivers, with a storage capacity that can absorb increased flow during a normal flood but can exacerbate problems during large floods. The dams also provide hydroelectric power, among the cleanest forms of energy. However, without proper soil conservation measures in the catchment areas, the accumulation of silt by soil erosion can severely limit a reservoir's life expectancy.

THE CARBON CYCLE

The geochemical carbon cycle is the transfer of carbon within the ecosphere, involving interactions between the crust, ocean, atmosphere, and life (Fig. 3-13). The biological carbon cycle, only a small component of the main cycle, is the transfer of carbon from the atmosphere to vegetation by photosynthesis, and then back to the atmosphere when plants respire or decay (Fig. 3-14). Only about a third of all chemical elements, mostly hydrogen, oxygen, carbon, and nitrogen, are recycled biologically.

The vast majority of carbon is not stored in living tissue but locked up in sedimentary rocks; even the amount of carbon contained in fossil fuels is meager by comparison. Nevertheless, the combustion of large quantities of fossil fuels and the destruction of the world's forests is transferring more carbon to the atmosphere than it can dispose of. In this way, humans are "short-circuiting" the carbon cycle.

Carbon dioxide presently comprises about 350 parts per million of the air molecules in the atmosphere, amounting to about 800 billion tons of

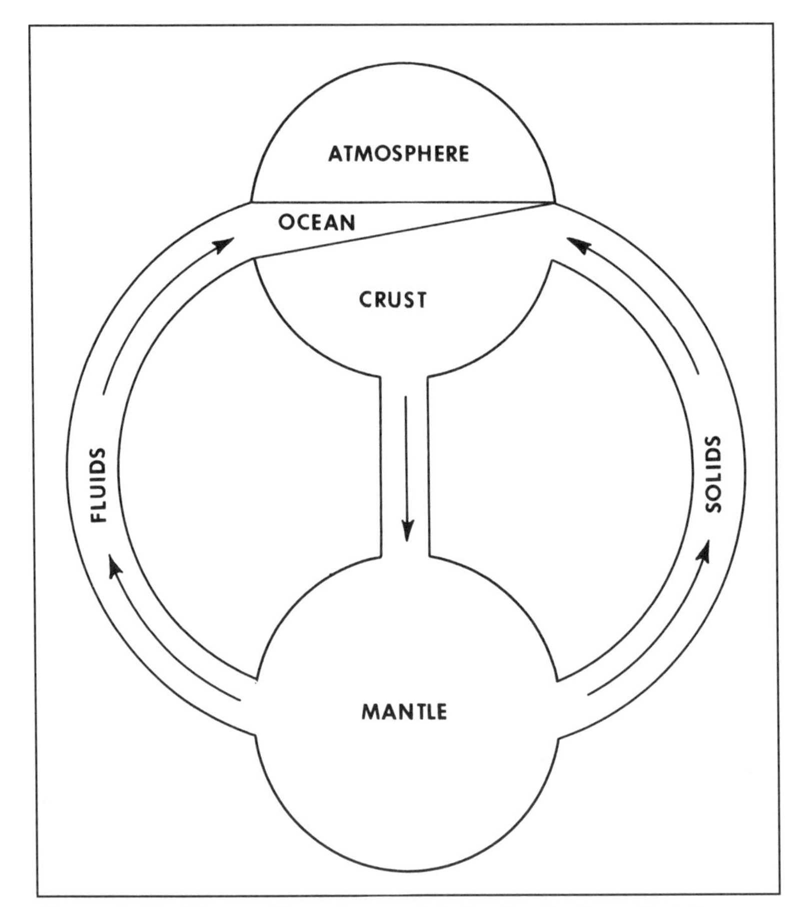

Figure 3–13 The cycling of materials in the Earth, called the geochemical carbon cycle.

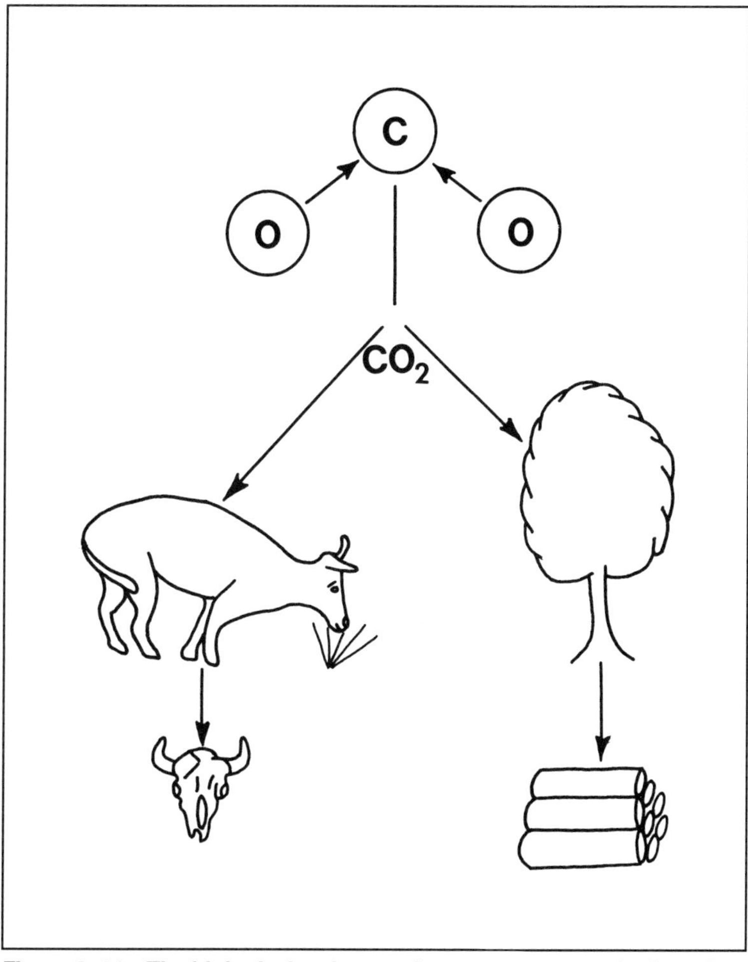

Figure 3–14 The biological carbon cycle converts atmospheric carbon dioxide directly into vegetative matter or indirectly into animal matter, which converts back to carbon dioxide upon decay or combustion.

carbon. It is one of the most important greenhouse gases, trapping solar heat that would otherwise escape into space, and operating somewhat like a thermostat to regulate the temperature of the planet. If the carbon cycle removes too much carbon dioxide, the Earth cools, if the carbon cycle generates too much carbon dioxide, the Earth warms. Therefore, even slight changes in the carbon cycle could considerably affect the climate.

The world's oceans play a vital role in regulating the level of carbon dioxide in the atmosphere. In the upper layers of the ocean, the concentration of gases is in equilibrium with the atmosphere. The mixed layer of the ocean—the top 250 feet (Fig. 3-15)—contains as much carbon dioxide as the entire atmosphere. The gas dissolves into the waters of the ocean mainly by the agitation of surface waves. If the ocean were without photosynthetic organisms to absorb dissolved carbon dioxide, much of its reservoir of this gas would escape into the atmosphere, more than tripling the present content.

Much of the carbon in the ocean comes from the land. Atmospheric carbon dioxide combines with rainwater to form carbonic acid. The acid reacts with surface rocks to produce dissolved calcium and bicarbonate that are carried by streams to the sea. Marine organisms use these substances to build their calcium carbonate skeletons and other supporting structures. When the organisms die, their skeletons sink to the ocean bottom, where they dissolve in the deep abyssal waters. The huge abyss contains the largest reservoir of carbon dioxide, holding 60 times more carbon than the entire atmosphere.

Sediments on the ocean floor and on the continents store most of the carbon. In shallow water, carbonate skeletons from once-living organisms build thick deposits of carbonate rock, such as limestone, and bury carbon in the crust. The burial of carbonate in this manner is responsible for about 80 percent of the carbon deposited on the ocean floor. The rest comes from the burial of dead organic matter washed off the continents.

Half of the bicarbonate in the ocean transforms back into carbon dioxide, which returns to the atmosphere, mostly by upwelling currents in the tropics. Therefore, the concentration of atmospheric carbon dioxide is highest near the equator. If it were not for this process, in 10,000 years all carbon dioxide would be removed from the atmosphere, and the loss of this

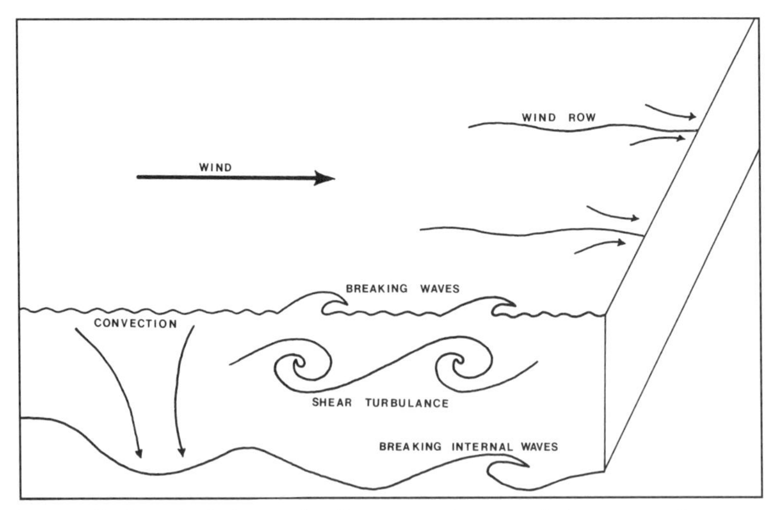

Figure 3–15 Turbulence in the upper layers of the ocean induces mixing of temperature, nutrients, and gases in the atmosphere.

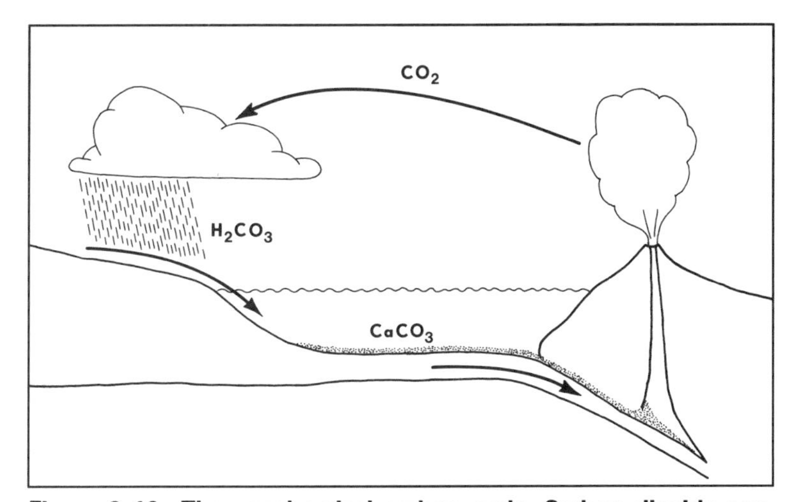

Figure 3–16 The geochemical carbon cycle. Carbon dioxide converted into bicarbonate is washed off the land and enters the ocean, where marine organisms convert it into carbonate sediments, which are thrust into the Earth's interior and become part of molten magma. Carbon dioxide is returned to the atmosphere by volcanic eruptions.

important greenhouse gas would result in the cessation of photosynthesis and the extinction of life.

Carbon is returned to the environment by oceanic and terrestrial volcanic activity. Volcanoes play an important role in restoring the carbon dioxide content of the atmosphere. The carbon dioxide escapes from carbonaceous sediments that melt in the Earth's interior to provide new magma for volcanoes. The molten magma along with its carbon dioxide rises to the surface to feed magma chambers beneath volcanoes. When the volcanoes erupt, carbon dioxide is released from the magma and returns to the atmosphere (Fig. 3-16).

THE NITROGEN CYCLE

About 80 percent of the atmosphere is composed of nitrogen, which is one of the major constituents of living matter. Carbon, nitrogen, and hydrogen are the essential elements for manufacturing proteins and other biological molecules. Nitrogen is practically an inert gas and requires special chemical reactions in order for nature to utilize it. Therefore, to make nitrogen combine with other substances, a great deal of energy is required.

The nitrogen cycle is a continuous exchange of elements between the atmosphere and the biosphere, spurred by the action of organisms such as nitrogen-fixing bacteria which metabolize atmospheric nitrogen for use by plants. All methods of nitrogen fixation, which converts nitrogen into useful chemicals, require an abundant source of energy, mainly supplied by the sun. The Earth also provides a source of energy in the form of hydrothermal vents on the deep ocean floor which are used by animals living near them to fix nitrogen for bacteria (Fig. 3-17). Plants and animals utilize large quantities of nitrogen incorporated in proteins. The decay of organisms after death releases nitrogen back into the atmosphere, thus forming a closed cycle.

Atmospheric nitrogen originated from early volcanic eruptions and the breakdown of ammonia, a molecule composed of one nitrogen atom and three hydrogen atoms and a large constituent of the primordial atmosphere. Unlike most other gases, which have been replaced or permanently stored in the crust, the Earth retains much of its original nitrogen, due to the presence of life forms that prevent nitrogen from transforming into nitrate,

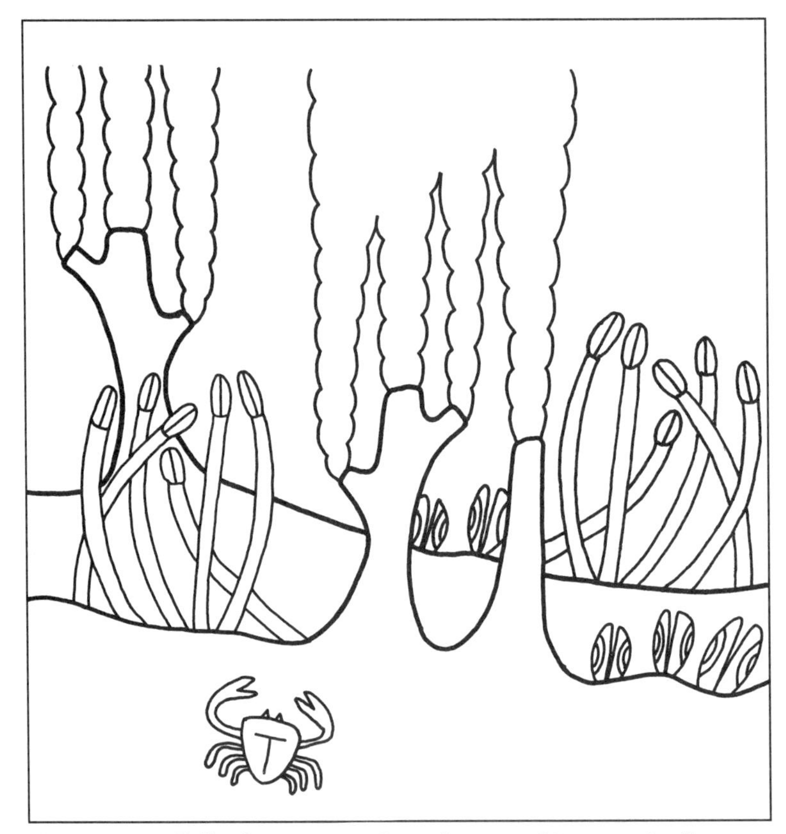

Figure 3–17 Tall tube worms, giant clams, and large crabs live near hydrothermal vents on the deep ocean floor.

a substance that is easily dissolved in the ocean. Instead denitrifying bacteria return the nitrate-nitrogen to its gaseous state. Without this process, all the nitrogen in the atmosphere would have disappeared long ago and the Earth would have only a fraction of its present atmospheric pressure.

Crops require large amounts of fixed nitrogen. However, the natural supply of fixed nitrogen is limited, imposing a limit on world agriculture. Therefore, supplemental nitrogen must be supplied by chemical fertilizers if agriculture is to keep up with the ever-expanding human population. Unfortunately, artificial fertilizers do not produce crops as nutritious as those grown using natural fertilizers, and countries that regularly rely on chemical fertilizers could end up with inadequate diets.

Today's high-yield crops quickly deplete the soil of fixed nitrogen, which must be replenished either by applying organic fertilizers—the preferred method—or chemical fertilizers, which require large amounts of energy in their manufacture, usually supplied by fossil fuels. In this light it is apparent that world agriculture, along with the people it feeds, would suffer catastrophically from a severe energy shortage. If humans are to survive well into the future, better agricultural methods must be developed and rapidly implemented.

4

ENVIRONMENTAL DEGRADATION

Perhaps no other species has had a more detrimental impact on this planet during its entire 4.5-billion-year existence than humans. The rapidly growing masses of people have inflicted major damage on the Earth in a relatively short time span. Our species is also largely responsible for many of the climatic disturbances that beset the planet. Since the Industrial Revolution of the mid 18th century, the composition of the atmosphere has changed significantly faster than at any other time in human history. In effect, we are conducting a global experiment by altering the environment with our waste products. We are destroying the world's forests and pumping pollutants into the air and water, thus unfavorably changing the composition of the biosphere.

GLOBAL POLLUTION

Pollution is so pervasive it requires solutions on a global scale. Pollutants discharged into the air and water are permanently altering the biosphere and affecting the global climate. As human populations continue to grow out of control, other species are pushed aside to make room for additional

Figure 4–1 Trash and debris strewn along the banks of the Brandywine River near Greenfield, Indiana. Photo by E. W. Cole, courtesy of USDA–Soil Conservation Service

agriculture, industry, and urbanization—activities that are all accompanied by habitat destruction.

The industrialization that made modern civilization possible is polluting the environment heavily (Fig. 4-1). The release of cancer-causing chemicals and other hazardous substances into the atmosphere and the ocean is far greater and more widespread than ever before suspected. Dangerous chemicals seep into groundwater supplies, placing many industrial municipalities at risk from contaminated drinking water. Each year, about 8 million tons of toxic wastes dumped into the ocean could cause irreversible changes in aquatic ecosystems.

Tropical forests are being destroyed for agriculture and timber harvest on an alarming scale. Some 100 acres of tropical forest are laid waste every minute, placing in jeopardy millions of plant and animal species. After the forests are leveled and abandoned, the ground becomes a barren wasteland. Improper farming techniques erode topsoil at several times the replacement rate, causing man-made deserts to spread throughout the world especially in Amazonia and Subsaharan Africa. In addition, natural deserts encroach on once-fertile agricultural lands. Strong winds send the sediment aloft, and huge dust storms clog the skies.

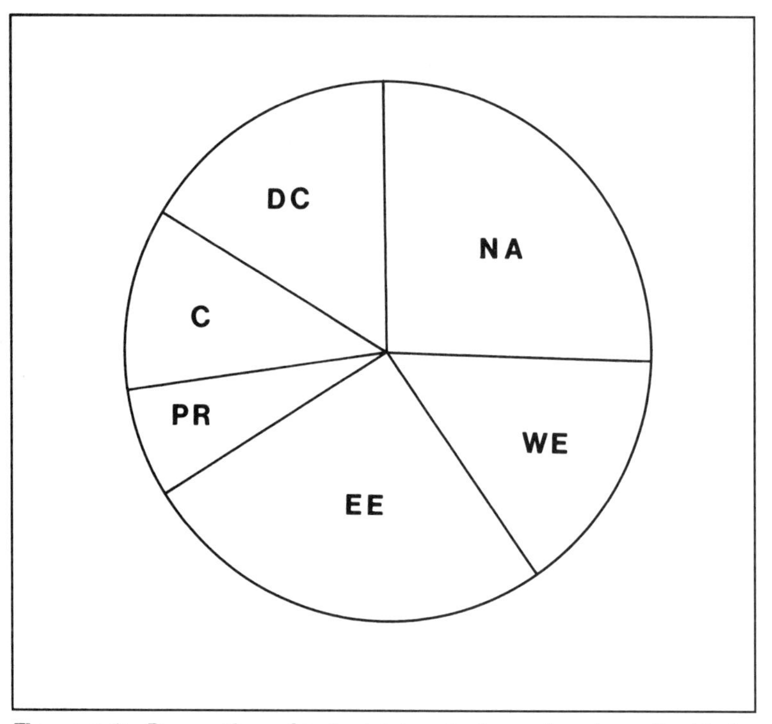

Figure 4–2 Proportion of industrial emissions of carbon dioxide by North America (NA), Western Europe (WE), Eastern Europe (EE), Pacific Rim (PM), China (C), and developing countries (DC).

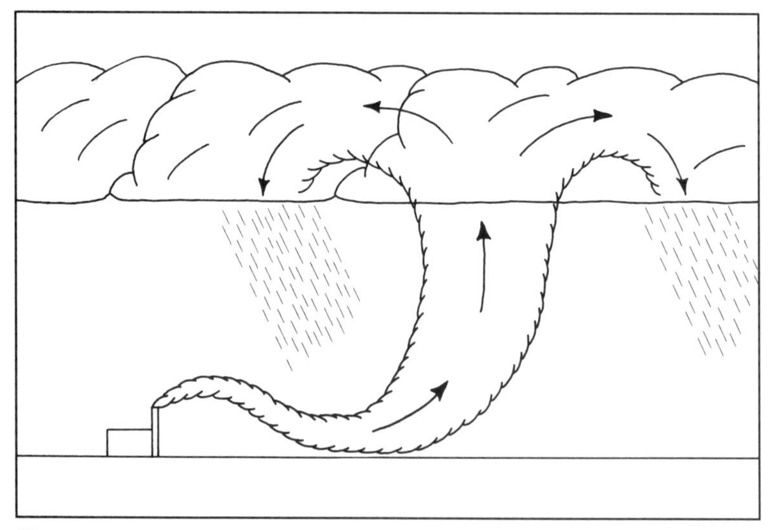

Figure 4–3 Acid rain production by cloud scavenging of air pollutants.

Massive quantities of carbon dioxide from the combustion of fossil fuels and the destruction of forests invade the atmosphere (Fig. 4-2). The continuation of these practices could raise global temperatures and adversely affect weather patterns, making some areas uninhabitable. Combustion of fossil fuels also produces deadly acid rain, a direct consequence of the self-cleaning nature of the atmosphere (Fig. 4-3). High acidity levels in the environment destroy forests, crops, fish, and much of the ancient buildings and other artifacts from earlier civilizations.

AIR POLLUTION

In November 1991, astronauts aboard the space shuttle *Atlantis* reported an amazing amount of haze covering the Earth, hampering their view of the surface. Since the industrial era began two centuries ago, our species has rivaled nature in disposing of toxic wastes and particulates into the atmosphere. Air pollution has become a growing threat to the world's health and welfare because of the ever-increasing emissions of contaminants into the atmosphere. In the United States, two-thirds of the population, or about 150 million people, live in areas where the air quality fails to meet the pollution standards set by the 1970 Clean Air Act.

TABLE 4–1 EMISSIONS OF CONTAMINANTS IN THE UNITED STATES (in millions of tons per year)

Source	Carbon Monoxide	Particulates	Sulfur Oxides	Hydrocarbons	Nitrogen Oxides
Transportation	92	1	1	12	10
Industry	9	12	29	13	15
Waste Disposal	3	1		1	
Other	5	1		4	
Total	109	15	30	30	25

The amount of particulate matter, soot, and dust suspended in the atmosphere as a result of human activities is estimated at about 15 million tons and is rapidly rising. Slash-and-burn agriculture destroys millions of acres of forest land each year and lofts tremendous amounts of smoke into the atmosphere. Dust storms in desert regions are on the rise. Wind-blown sediment from newly plowed or abandoned fields clogs the atmosphere and severely erodes the land (Fig. 4-4). Nearly half of the world's croplands are losing topsoil at rates that undermine future productivity.

Figure 4–4 A 1935 dust storm in Baca County, Colorado, where it was as dark as midnight for over an hour. Photo by K. Welch, courtesy of USDA–Soil Conservation Service

Factory and power plant smokestacks expel massive quantities of soot and aerosols—minute liquid and solid particles mainly produced by chemical processes resulting from the combustion of fossil fuels, which are essentially acidic. Motor vehicle exhaust accounts for half the particulates and aerosols injected into the atmosphere. Millions of pounds of known carcinogens (cancer-causing agents) are spewed into the atmosphere each year. Factories around the world send aloft thousands of tons of dangerous chemicals annually. Many of these substances rain out of the atmosphere and contaminate soil and water, where they can concentrate to toxic levels.

Human industrial activities release 10 times more sulfur into the atmosphere than natural sources like volcanoes. Most of the sulfur compounds originate from the combustion of high sulfur coal and oil, along with the smelting of sulfide ores, from which metals are extracted, particularly in the heavily industrialized regions of the Northern Hemisphere. The sulfate particles are often highly acidic and can damage materials and alter the pH balance of rivers and lakes and damage forests. Sulfates are the leading constituents of acid rain and can cut visibility in half by scattering and absorbing sunlight, leaving many industrial centers living in a persistent haze.

The atmosphere's cleansing agent is a short-lived molecule composed of one hydrogen atom and one oxygen atom, called hydroxyl, which strongly reacts with most atmospheric contaminants, rendering them harmless. Unfortunately, with the mounting load of atmospheric pollutants—mostly carbon monoxide and methane—caused by human activities, the amount of hydroxyl is declining just when it is needed the most. Since the beginning of the industrial era, hydroxyl has decreased as much as 20 percent. Further declines could mean much dirtier skies in the future.

In many areas, precipitation has changed since the beginning of the industrial era from a nearly neutral solution to a dilute solution of sulfuric and nitric acid. In the most extreme cases, the rain has the acidity of vinegar. Even virtually unindustrialized areas, like the tropics, are plagued with acid rain, mainly from burning rain forests. Some lakes and streams have been made so acidic by acid rain runoff or are so polluted by toxic wastes that fish populations have been almost totally decimated (Fig. 4-5). Acid rain kills simple organisms and other creatures further up the aquatic food chain.

Figure 4–5 Fish killed by the pollution of Frene Creek, Hermann County, Missouri from an unknown source on August 1, 1971. The estimated kill was 10,000 to 15,000 fish. Courtesy of USDA–Soil Conservation Service

Figure 4–6 Smoke and refuse from garbage incineration cause considerable land, air, and water pollution near Brunswick, Maine. Photo by Richard Duncan, courtesy of USDA–Soil Conservation Service

Acid runoff, along with direct deposition of acid rain, taints once-pristine lakes with levels of mercury high enough to be a public health risk. Mercury also descends upon lakes as fallout from distant sources such as coal-fired electrical generating plants, smelters, and incinerators (Fig. 4-6). Many lakes in the United States, Canada, and Sweden harbor fish populations with concentrations of mercury well above federally permissible limits. The fish are relatively unaffected by low levels of mercury and can accumulate substantial amounts without serious ill effects. However, higher animals like mammals and humans can suffer adverse health effects by eating mercury-tainted fish. Furthermore, mercury, like most toxins, concentrates to higher levels as it moves up the food chain, as larger species consume smaller ones.

Acid rain, which damages vegetation by harming foliage and root systems, is adversely affecting agricultural crops and destroying the great forests of North America, Europe, and China (Fig. 4-7). Resorts and wilderness areas like those in the western United States, Norway, and West Germany are losing much of their natural beauty because of the destruction wrought by acid rain. Mountain forests are particularly at risk when covered by acid clouds, because the cloud base is usually more acidic than the acid rain itself.

Figure 4–7 Areas of heavy acid precipitation in the world.

One of the greatest surprises of this century has been the discovery of a huge ozone hole over Antarctica, where half the stratospheric ozone disappears during the southern winter (Fig. 4-8).

Ozone, which constitutes less than one part per million of the gases in the atmosphere, performs a vital function by shielding the Earth from the

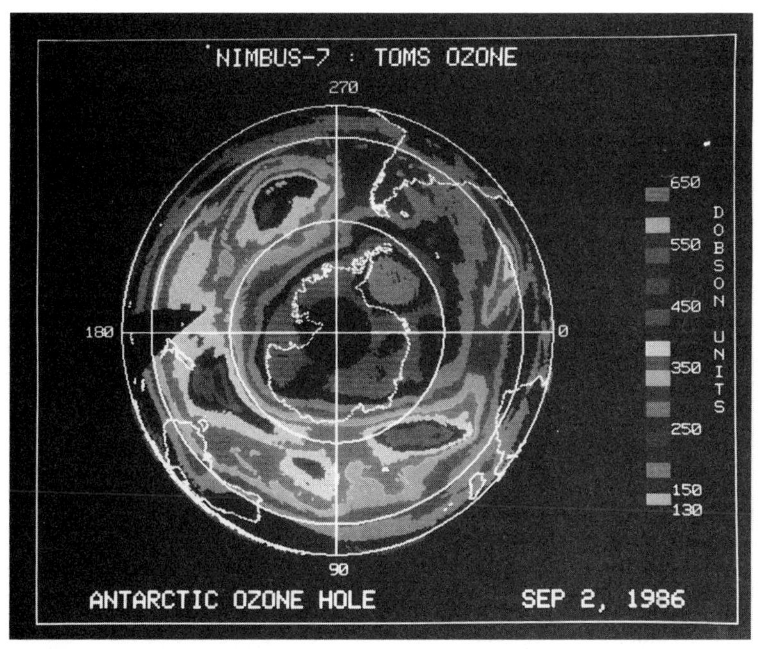

Figure 4–8 A map of total ozone in the Southern Hemisphere from *Nimbus 7* satellite illustrating the Antarctic ozone hole. Courtesy of NASA

sun's harmful shortwave ultraviolet radiation (Fig. 4-9). Without this shield, life could not exist on land or in the surface waters of the ocean.

When the ozone hole breaks up in the spring, ozone-depleted air travels to the mid-latitudes, where ultraviolet levels climb appreciably. A similar ozone hole often hovers over the Arctic, jeopardizing parts of the Northern Hemisphere with high ultraviolet exposures. The ozone shield over the United States is eroding twice as fast as had been previously predicted. Long-term records show that ozone levels in the high northern latitudes have dropped about 5 percent over the last two decades and could drop another 5 percent early in the next century. Each percentage point drop in the level of ozone could result in a 2 percent rise in the incidence of skin cancer.

The ozone depletion is strongly believed to be caused by man-made chemicals, principally halocarbons used as refrigerants and solvents, along with nitrogen oxides from the combustion of fossil fuels and deforestation. Extreme cold conditions in the polar stratosphere help pollution destroy ozone by chemical processes. In addition, large volcanic eruptions, like Mount Pinatubo's in the Philippines in June 1991, contribute to ozone depletion by emitting sulfuric acid. Unfortunately, even if the chemical emissions ceased entirely, the ozone layer would continue to diminish for at least another century—the amount of time required to cleanse the upper

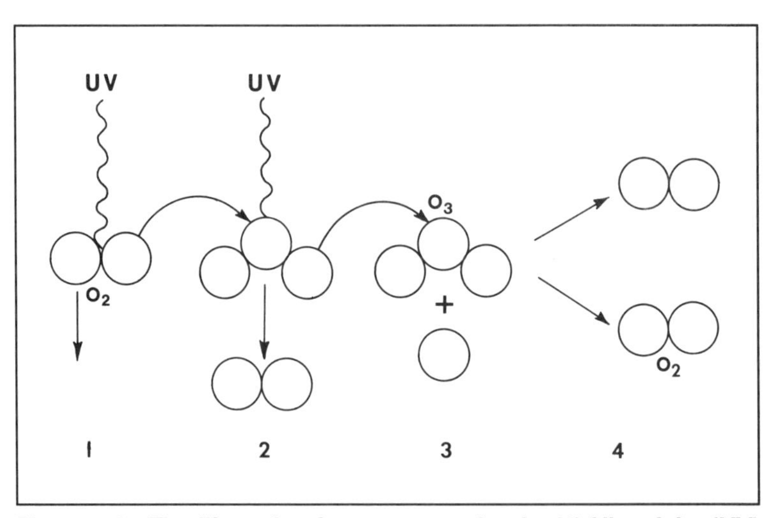

Figure 4-9 The life cycle of an ozone molecule. (1) Ultraviolet (UV) radiation splits an oxygen molecule into 2 oxygen atoms. (2) One of these atoms combines with another oxygen molecule to create an ozone molecule. The ozone molecule traps UV, liberating an oxygen molecule and an oxygen atom, to reform as an ozone molecule. (3) The addition of another oxygen atom creates (4) two new oxygen molecules.

atmosphere of ozone-destroying chemicals. Meanwhile, exposure to sunlight would have to be limited in order to reduce the risk of cancer and other illnesses.

A slight increase in ultraviolet radiation can promote a rise in medical conditions such as skin cancer, cataracts, and weakened immune systems, as well as harming animals and plants—especially crops needed to sustain an ever-growing human population. High levels of ultraviolet radiation could also exacerbate serious pollution problems such as smog and acid rain. A continued depletion of the ozone layer with accompanying high ultraviolet exposures could destroy the primary producers at the bottom of the food chain that are critical to all life.

WATER POLLUTION

The world's oceans cover an area of about 140 million square miles and contain over 300 million cubic miles of seawater. Such a vast quantity of water would seem impervious to human pollution. Yet in many coastal areas worldwide toxic chemicals pour into rivers and streams (Fig. 4-10),

Figure 4–10 A broken sewage pipe pollutes the Mississippi River near Bemidji, Minnesota. Photo by C. H. Aubol, courtesy of USDA–Soil Conservation Service

and untreated or partially treated sewage flows directly into the ocean, where it becomes a menace to life. As a result, beaches in many parts of the world are unsightly and unsafe. The importance of water to life is obvious, but too often this factor is overlooked. As a result, much of the surface and subsurface water is polluted by human activities. The accumulation of toxic substances in the ocean from runoff could cause irreparable damage to the marine environment.

The world's rivers and coastal waters have become the dumping grounds for millions of tons of toxic wastes yearly. In addition, raw sewage from coastal treatment plants sometimes drains into the sea because of overflow or equipment failure during heavy downpours along the American East Coast as well as other heavily populated coastal regions. Some of these toxic pollutants like PCPs and human excrement are powerful carcinogens and mutagens. Others, nonbiodegradable pollutants such as plastics, persist in the environment for long periods. Ocean currents bring the wastes back to shore, and some wastes

Figure 4–11a Aerial view of the December 19, 1976, *Argo Merchant* oil spill 28 miles off the coast of Nantucket, Massachusetts. Courtesy of NASA

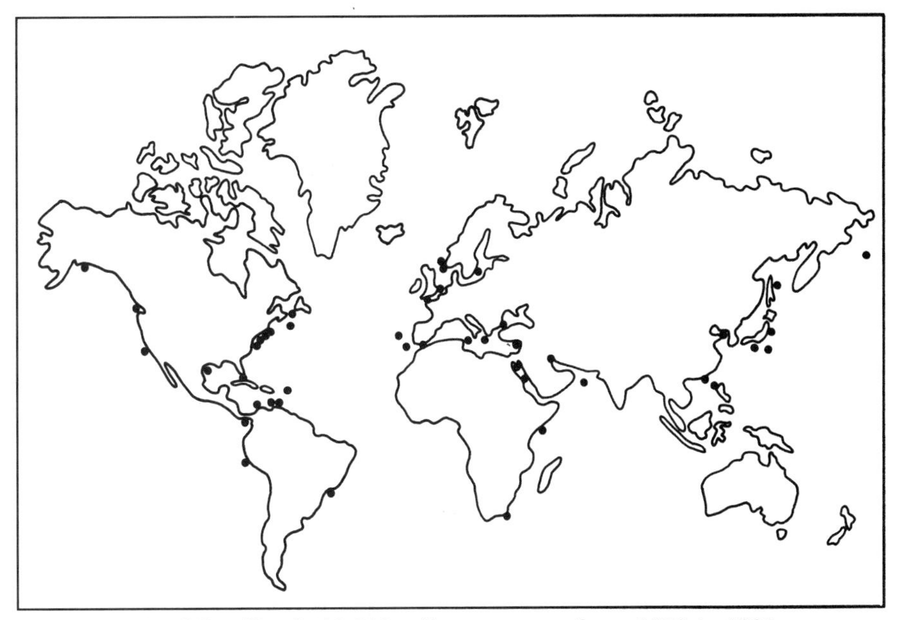

Figure 4–11b Oil spills of 100,000 gallons or more from 1989 to 1991.

concentrate between thermal layers and ocean fronts, some of which are the world's most productive fishing grounds.

Much of the waste that falls to the bottom of the ocean is highly toxic. Some 250 dead dolphins washed ashore along the Atlantic coast of the United States in the summer of 1987. A mysterious epidemic killed more than 7,000 seals in the heavily polluted North Sea in 1988. Other dead marine animals wash up on shore by the thousands, and fishermen report large hauls of dead fish. Coastal sewage and industrial toxins are a prime suspect in these deaths. Realizing the serious threat to the nation's coastal waters, in 1988 the United States enacted legislation banning all ocean dumping by 1992. Unfortunately, the sludge on the bottom of the ocean from previous decades of dumping remains a serious hazard to marine life.

The coastal seas of the world are among the most fragile and sensitive environments. Some changes that human activity has caused in the ocean environment are irreversible. These activities include damming rivers, which lessens discharge into the sea, and building ports at the mouths of estuaries, which permanently changes the patterns of water flow and alters coastal habitats.

By far the most damaging of all sources of coastal and river pollution are oil spills (Figs. 4-11a&b). Increasing demand for offshore oil, collisions and groundings of oil tankers and barges, attacks on oil tankers by belligerent nations, and the deliberate dumping of oil into the sea during the 1991 Persian Gulf war all have disastrous ecological consequences. Every year,

as much as 25 million barrels of oil spill into the world's oceans. Offshore drilling and shipping accidents account for some 20 million tons of dissolved and suspended matter in the ocean, which affects coastal zones most dramatically.

Contamination of the groundwater supply has become the primary environmental challenge of the century. Toxic chemicals leach out of thousands of landfills in the United States. Agricultural pesticides, herbicides, and fertilizers penetrate into the ground, and contaminants percolate downward through layers of soil into groundwater aquifers. Man-made organic chemicals, heavy metals, and other toxic substances also seep into the groundwater system. These toxins could contaminate aquifers to such an extent that in the ensuing years half the nation's groundwater would be rendered unsafe. Already, as much as 10 percent of the groundwater supply across the United States is heavily contaminated.

WASTE DISPOSAL

The disposal of mounting piles of waste generated by modern society remains one of the most perverse problems we face in the upcoming years (Fig. 4-12). Landfills in most major cities are overflowing, and few new spaces are available in which to put the trash. As the number of dump sites

Figure 4–12 Americans dispose of 250 million automobile tires each year. Shown here are old tires embedded in bay mud of tidal flats on the east side of San Francisco Bay, California. Photo by D. H. Radbruch, courtesy of USGS

Figure 4–13 Rocky Flats nuclear materials production plant, Golden, Colorado.
Courtesy of U.S. Department of Energy

dwindles, the garbage continues to mount, while the growing population keeps on generating waste. Much of the garbage is composed of nonbiodegradable materials, like plastic, and remains in the environment for a long time. Most of the waste is trucked to already overflowing landfills and buried under conditions that do not allow it to deteriorate properly.

Because of the high cost of the disposal of toxic wastes on land, coastal metropolitan areas worldwide dump municipal and industrial wastes directly into the sea. Much of the waste that washes to shore comes from overburdened sewage-treatment plants, accidental spills by garbage barges, and lack of winds to disperse the flotsam. Often, untreated sewage is dumped directly into the ocean by overflows caused by floods. Along with human effluent, other municipal wastes are disposed of in metropolitan sewage systems, with the potential of environmental damage and the spread of diseases, often resulting in beach closings in many parts of the world.

The disposal of radioactive wastes from nuclear power plants, hospital radiation labs, and nuclear weapons manufacturing facilities (Fig. 4-13) is of great concern because of the expansion of nuclear technology throughout the world and uncertainties about its long-term environmental effects. As human populations continue to grow and the demand for nuclear-generated electricity rises, a viable solution for the storage of nuclear wastes will have to be found; otherwise, there will be an overreliance on fossil fuels, along with the enormous pollution problems this entails.

ENVIRONMENTAL RESTORATION

Annually, Americans generate nearly 600 million tons of hazardous waste and wastewater, requiring up to $80 billion for disposal and treatment. During 1990, the United States spent over $100 billion, about 2 percent of it gross domestic product, on environmental cleanup. Over 1,000 sites on the U.S. Environmental Protection Agency's national priority list have been slated for cleanup (Fig. 4-14), a number that is likely to double before this century is out.

The sources of pollution are so diverse that determining the major cause of groundwater contamination is often difficult. Routine monitoring of industrial waste lagoons and landfills reveals that the chemicals are not being contained and are contaminating nearby water wells, forcing many residents across the country to rely on bottled drinking water. The cost of cleaning the toxic sites is phenomenally expensive, requiring huge sums of money from the U.S. Environmental Protection Agency's Superfund.

The contamination of aquifers by toxic chemicals requires the testing of nearby water wells. After the pollution has been located, determining its

Figure 4–14 Location of major dump sites and aquifers identified for cleanup by the U.S. Environmental Protection Agency.

Figure 4–15 A Forest Service biologist checks an area that was cleaned by Exxon workers using high-pressure hot water, following the 1989 Alaskan oil spill. Photo by Jill Bauermeister, courtesy of U.S. Forest Service

extent is often difficult and expensive, and in many cases, cleanup is nearly impossible. If the contamination is irreversible, the water must be treated at the wellhead, at great cost. Most states that bear the burden of monitoring and safeguarding the groundwater cannot afford the enormous expenditures without federal support.

The cleanup of landfills and waste lagoons is also expensive. Bioremediation, which utilizes microbes to digest toxic wastes, can be used to clean up soil that has been contaminated by underground storage tanks. But the only remedial action for soils contaminated with toxic or radioactive wastes is to transport them to hazardous waste dumps. Ultimately, improved methods of dealing with waste problems and better knowledge of the underground environment can help solve future problems. Unfortunately for much of the nation's groundwater supply, past mistakes might have made recovery impossible.

At sea, combating oil spills requires containment, using floating booms or an absorbent material such as straw. Burning the oil eliminates most of the pollution if it is done soon after the spill and before it spreads or coagulates with seawater. If the oil washes to shore, a labor-intensive cleanup is required (Fig. 4-15). Detergents or other chemicals can break up and disperse the oil, but many of these chemicals are toxic and can cause additional ecological damage. Cleaning up oil-soaked beaches requires

Figure 4–16 Clean coal technology demonstrated at the Yates electrical generation station, Coweta County, Georgia. Courtesy of U.S. Department of Energy

chemical dispersants or steam, which kill organisms that otherwise would have survived if left alone. Often, nature does a better job of cleaning up oil-soaked beaches than people do.

Acid precipitation can be reduced by installing scrubbers on coal-fired plant smokestacks and by using low-sulfur coal to eliminate sulfur dioxide (Fig. 4-16). Many coal-fired electrical generating plants could convert to natural gas, which is a much cleaner-burning fuel, producing only half the amount of carbon that coal does per unit of energy. Nevertheless, even if acid precipitation ends today, years or perhaps decades could elapse before the environment recovers. Furthermore, many older plants built before 1975, and many plants built in other countries, are not required to make these costly investments. Governments are generally reluctant to pass laws requiring mandatory emission controls for cleaning up the environment because of possible adverse economic effects.

Some 250 lakes and 25,000 miles of streams in the United States have higher-than-normal acidity levels (Fig. 4-17). Many sensitive aquatic species die from long-term exposure to low acidity levels or short-term exposure to high acidity levels. High acidity levels in lakes and streams can be treated with lime made from limestone, which neutralizes the acids, though treating the watersheds that feed the streams and lakes is more effective than applying the lime directly. Furthermore, halting acid precip-

Figure 4–17 Areas where streams and lakes are highly acidified in the United States.

itation at the source by treating the flue gases at coal-fired plants with lime could clear up half the acidic surface waters.

Curtailing the depletion of the ozone layer is more difficult. Many nations are discontinuing the use of refrigerants and solvents containing chlorofluorocarbons (CFCs), which devour ozone molecules; however, many other countries are slow to take action. Meanwhile, the ozone layer continues to be ravaged.

5

RESOURCE DEPLETION

The Western world is devouring natural resources at a rapid rate. Only one-fifth of the human population lives in the relatively few rich nations of the Northern Hemisphere, while four-fifths inhabit poverty-stricken countries, mainly in the Southern Hemisphere, often referred to as the "poor South." The rich nations consume about 80 percent of the Earth's natural resources, however, and are directly or indirectly responsible for most of the pollution and degradation of the environment.

An increase in the efficiency of energy use and the utilization of alternative fuels would help improve the environments of the developed nations. Such an effort also would help the developing countries raise their standards of living without a significant increase in energy use and a corresponding rise in pollution. Failure to take these measures could condemn most of the human population to inhumane living conditions.

FOSSIL FUELS

Petroleum supplies nearly half the world's energy (Fig. 5-1). Of the over one trillion barrels of oil thus far discovered, the sources of fully a third or more have been exhausted. Daily, the world consumes about 65 million

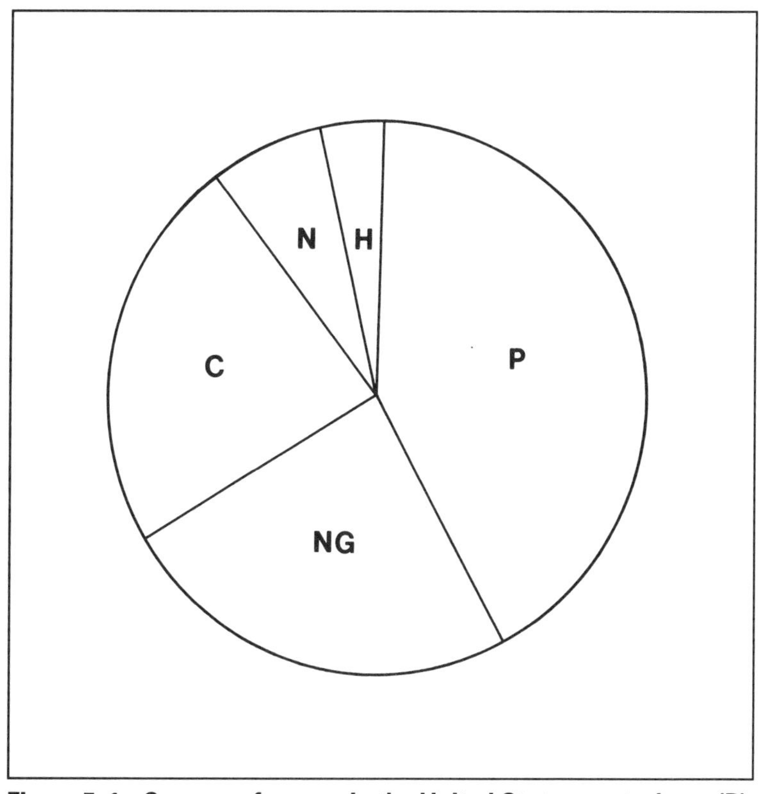

Figure 5–1 Sources of energy in the United States—petroleum (P), natural gas (NG), coal (C), nuclear (N), hydroelectric (H).

barrels of oil. The United States consumes about 17 million barrels of oil per day, or about a quarter of the world's total. The average European or Japanese uses between 10 and 30 barrels of oil annually, compared with over 40 barrels a year consumed by the average American. In contrast, the average person in a developing country uses the equivalent of only one or two barrels of oil a year. As a result of this disparity, developed nations pollute the environment considerably more than undeveloped countries do, even considering the latter's much greater cumulative population (representing 4 out of 5 of all the world's people).

About 20 percent of the world's oil and 5 percent of its natural gas production is from offshore sources (Fig. 5-2). Future projections indicate that twice as much oil will be pumped from offshore than from land. Unfortunately, a great deal of offshore oil spills into the ocean, amounting to as much as 2 million tons a year. These oil spills could create an enormous environmental problem as production rises.

Figure 5–2 An offshore drilling and production platform. Photo by M. V. Adams, courtesy of USGS

World energy consumption is expected to increase more than 50 percent by the year 2010, at which time petroleum supplies might fail to meet the increasing demand from growing industrialization. Oil production could eventually level off and begin to decline early in the next century. As a result, alternative fuels would have to be developed to meet the continuing demand for energy. Oil importing countries, which consume about half the oil on the market, would require a transition from a dependence on oil to a greater reliance on other fossil fuels, nuclear energy, and renewable energy sources.

Without reliable reserves, the United States could become dangerously dependent on foreign sources for meeting its demand. During the 1991

Persian Gulf war, the United States responded to the threat of a possible interruption in the global oil supply with the greatest military deployment since World War II. The large military expenditures by the United States and its allies underline how dependent Western economies have become on imported oil. The United States imports more than half its petroleum, a situation that could be disastrous to its economy if even a fraction of the imported oil were to be cut off. If military expenditures needed to protect the flow of oil worldwide are added to the true cost of petroleum, American motorists would pay two to three times more for gasoline than they now do.

Since the Industrial Revolution, energy consumption has risen exponentially (Fig. 5-3). The consumption of petroleum in industrialized nations is expected to increase significantly over the next 30 years. In addition, developing countries pursue industrialization to improve their standards of living. At the present rate of consumption, the easily tapped petroleum reserves could become exhausted by the year 2035. Unless some safe alternatives such as fission, fusion, solar, and geothermal energy are developed and rapidly exploited, industrial plants might have to convert to coal, whose resources have barely been touched, but whose environmental impact is much more severe.

Coal supplies about a quarter of the world's energy. The peak usage was during the 1920s, when coal accounted for more than 70 percent of fuel consumption and most air pollution (Fig. 5-4). The United States has increased its coal consumption by about 70 percent since the 1970s, mostly for coal-fired electrical generation. Electrical generating plants account for

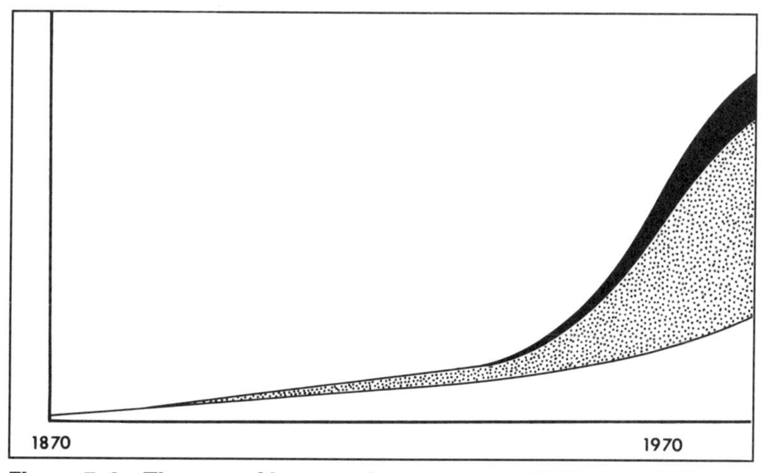

Figure 5–3 The rate of increase in energy use. White area indicates coal use, stippled area indicates oil and gas use, and black area indicates electricity use.

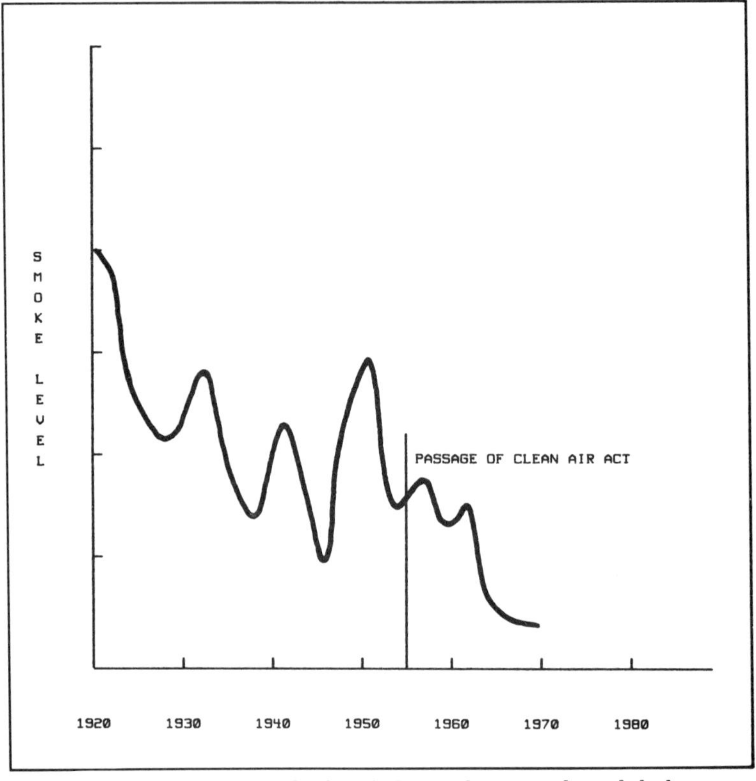

Figure 5–4 Relative smoke levels have decreased, mainly because of conversion from coal to petroleum.

about 75 percent of the coal consumed in the U.S., and coal-fired power plants provide nearly 60 percent of America's electrical energy.

The coal from Eastern underground mines (Fig. 5-5) generally has a high sulfur content, requiring the installation of smokestack scrubbers on coal-fired power plants to cut emissions of sulfur products that cause acid rain. Alternatively, utilities could burn low-sulfur Western coal, which is mined mostly from massive open pits (Fig. 5-6). To keep up with an increasing demand, the United States would have to mine about 60 percent more coal by the turn of the century.

The annual world coal production is about 5 billion tons, with the United States accounting for about half that amount. Coal reserves far exceed those of all other fossil fuels combined and are sufficient to support a large increase in consumption well into the next century. Economically recoverable reserves—those reserves able to be reached without incurring prohibative costs—are estimated at nearly a trillion tons, and at the present rate of consumption, coal could possibly last another two centuries.

Figure 5–5 Underground coal mining near Benton, Illinois. Courtesy of U.S. Department of Energy

Figure 5–6 Open pit coal mining at the Absaloka mine, Montana. Courtesy of USGS

Since the United States possesses nearly half the world's economically recoverable reserves, coal could become the most likely alternative fuel to replace petroleum when supplies run low. Unfortunately, coal combustion yields twice as much carbon dioxide per unit of energy as oil and natural gas. Therefore, a dramatic changeover to coal could contribute substantially to the greenhouse effect, which influences the global climate.

The long-term increase in atmospheric carbon dioxide, as much as 25 percent since 1860, is the result of an accelerated release of carbon dioxide by fossil fuel combustion. For every ton of carbon in fossil fuels, over 3.5 tons of carbon dioxide is liberated during combustion. The present consumption of fossil fuels yields on average about 1.1 tons of atmospheric carbon for each person on Earth annually. Americans release nearly 6 tons per person yearly, amounting to about 1.5 billion tons, or about a quarter of the world's total. If the consumption of fossil fuel continues at its present furious pace, economically recoverable reserves could go up in smoke in just a few decades.

ORE DEPOSITS

We live in a world rich in natural resources, and the exploitation of minerals and energy has greatly improved people's lives. Unfortunately, the depletion of natural resources could threaten future advancement. We are depleting fossil fuels thousands of times faster than their rate of formation. Many high-grade ore deposits have been heavily exploited and might soon be mined out. The consumption of mineral ores to maintain a

TABLE 5–1 NATURAL RESOURCE LEVELS

	Depletion Rate in Years at Present Consumption	
Commodity	**Reserves***	**Total Resources**
Aluminum	250	800
Coal	200	3,000
Platinum	225	400
Cobalt	100	400
Molybdenum	65	250
Nickel	65	160
Copper	40	270
Petroleum	35	80

* Reserves are resources recoverable with today's technology.

high standard of living in the industrialized world and to improve the quality of life in developing countries might lead to the depletion of known high-grade ore reserves by the middle of the next century. Then low-grade deposits would have to be worked, dramatically increasing the cost of goods and commodities.

Fortunately, we have barely scratched the surface in the search for mineral deposits. Immense resources lie at great depths, awaiting the mining technology to recover them. Huge untapped reserves of oil exist in oil-shale deposits in the Western United States (Fig. 5-7), with a potential oil content exceeding that of all other petroleum resources in the entire world. Large tar sand deposits, such as those in Alberta, Canada and in California, are another potential source of petroleum equal to about half a trillion barrels of oil, once they become economically viable. Most of the world's coal deposits are practically untouched. Abundant coal reserves exist in the western United States, Canada, Russia, China, and South Africa.

Iron ore exists in economically recoverable deposits on all continents. Layered deposits of iron oxide cover huge regions, such as the Hamersley Range of Western Australia and the Lake Superior region of North America. The Mesabi Range of northeast Minnesota is the major supplier of iron ore for the United States. The iron is contained in a banded iron formation that was laid down over 2 billion years ago. The Clinton iron formation is the

Figure 5–7 An outcrop of oil shale, Uintah County, Utah. Courtesy of USGS

Figure 5–8 The Duval Sulphur and Potash Company's mining operation near Carlsbad, New Mexico. Photo by E. F. Patterson, courtesy of USGS

chief iron producer in the Appalachian region. The iron is contained in an oolithic ironstone deposited over 400 million years ago. With today's technology, ore grades generally must exceed 30 percent in order for mining to be profitable.

Economically recoverable deposits of copper, lead, zinc, silver, and gold exist in the cordilleran mountain regions of North and South America. A variety of other metallic deposits lies in the mountains of southern Europe and in the mountain ranges of southern Asia as well. The world's largest nickel deposit is at Sudbury, Canada. Zambia's great copper belt is estimated to contain a quarter of the world's copper. Half the world's production of chromium comes from South Africa, which is also responsible for much of the global diamond production. The major platinum deposits of the world include the Bushveld Complex of South Africa and the Stillwater Complex of Montana. Rich lead and zinc hydrothermal deposits (emplaced by hot water) exist in the tri-state region of the Mississippi River Valley.

Important reserves of phosphate used for fertilizers are mined in Idaho and adjacent states. Evaporate deposits in the interiors of continents, such as the potassium deposits near Carlsbad, New Mexico (Fig. 5-8), indicate that these areas were once inundated by an ancient sea. Thick beds of gypsum used in the manufacture of plaster of paris and dry wall board also were deposited in the continental interiors. Nonmetallic minerals such as sand and gravel, clay, salt, and limestone are mined in large quantities throughout the world and have contributed substantially to the growth of civilization.

CONSERVATION

In the United States, industrial energy consumption per unit of production, per capita consumption of resources, and production of pollution are up to four times greater than for other modern industrial nations. A marked improvement in energy efficiency could cut industrial air pollution by upwards of 50 percent. By improving insulation and using more efficient appliances and lighting in buildings and homes, energy consumption and air pollution in those facilities can be cut by 50 percent or more.

Buildings are the single largest consumer of energy in the United States, comprising 40 percent of the total energy budget. Buildings consume three-quarters of all electricity generated in this country. Over a building's life span, the energy bill can add up to more than twice the construction cost. By using insulation and efficient construction materials and appliances, energy consumption in buildings could be reduced by half, saving the nation $200 billion a year.

Transportation sources consume about 200 billion gallons of fuel each year. They also produce over half the air pollution generated by the combustion of fossil fuels. An improvement of 5 miles per gallon in American automobile mileage would cut carbon dioxide emissions by nearly 100 million tons a year. Energy-efficient automobiles including electric vehicles (Fig. 5-9) would cut automotive carbon dioxide by up to 70 percent. Car pooling and greater reliance on mass transit would reduce smog in big cities. Furthermore, the use of alternative fuels such as natural gas and methanol would cut emissions, while lessening dependence on foreign sources of petroleum.

Coal is the most abundant hydrocarbon fuel, providing enough economically recoverable reserves at present rate of consumption to last two centuries. Unfortunately, it is also the dirtiest fuel in terms of emissions of particulate matter and carbon dioxide, along with aerosols composed of nitrogen and sulfur oxides that produce acid rain. However, coal is utilized more efficiently in pressurized, fluidized bed boilers, which use powered coal suspended in air. They burn most of the pollutants, cut nitrogen oxides by 30 percent, and reduce sulfur emissions by nearly 95 percent compared to conventional power plants. Moreover, pollution controls installed on existing coal-fired power plants could cut nitrogen oxides and sulfur dioxides by another 90 percent. The utilization of these technologies has significantly reduced acid rain in the United States relative to the 1970s and 1980s.

Figure 5-9 Electric vehicle development at the General Electric Research and Development Center, Schenectady, New York. Courtesy of U.S. Department of Energy

Natural gas composed mostly of methane is the second most plentiful hydrocarbon energy source in the nation. Switching to natural gas where possible would cut carbon dioxide emissions in half. Unfortunately, significant amounts of natural gas leak into the atmosphere during pipeline transmission and urban distribution, possibly contributing to greenhouse warming. Electrical generating plants and motor vehicles could take advantage of this fuel; compressed natural gas mixed with hydrogen yields the cleanest-burning alternative fuel for powering motor vehicles. Present reserves of natural gas can withstand steep increases well into the next century. Natural gas also could be supplemented with methane generated by the conversion of waste products (Fig. 5-10).

Figure 5–10 A facility designed to convert animal wastes into methane gas, Barton, Florida. Courtesy of U.S. Department of Energy

Instead of burning fuel in separate plants to generate electricity and manufacture products or heat buildings, efficiency is significantly improved if operations are combined in a process called cogeneration, which uses the heat rather than allowing it to simply escape into the atmosphere. Cogeneration could boost total efficiency by up to 90 percent and reduce air pollution by 40 to 50 percent. These conservation methods could curtail the effects of global climate change by improving energy efficiency and developing nonpolluting substitute energy sources. With the conservation of natural resources and the exploration of alternative energy sources, the wealth of the world can be preserved for future generations.

RECYCLING

Daily, Americans dispose of about 160 million tons of garbage. One method of dealing with the enormous garbage disposal problem has been to build expensive waste incinerators, sometimes using the heat to generate electricity. Unfortunately, as the waste disposal problem is solved, an enormous air pollution problem is created. A more acceptable solution to the growing disposal problem is recycling, combined with a concurrent reduction of convenience packaging and redundant products. Recycling reduces the amount of trash in landfills and generates no pollution; it also decreases the need to mine or harvest new raw materials, thereby helping to save the environment. Recycling also reduces the need for incineration and the pollution it entails.

Over three-quarters of the nation's municipal solid waste is recyclable material. However, implementing recycling on a national scale is difficult. The problem is that some industries refuse to use secondary materials. There is little economic incentive for recycling when alternative methods of waste disposal, such as incineration, abound. Unfortunately, incineration engenders a serious pollution problem. Every 100 tons of trash produces 30 tons of ash, which contains heavy metals and thereby qualifies as a hazardous waste. But incineration could be minimized or avoided entirely by aggressive recycling. The recycling of waste plastics, which account for about 40 percent of landfill trash, can yield a high-quality fuel oil to reduce the need for petroleum imports.

In order to reduce the amount of garbage, our economy, based as it is on overconsumption and waste, would have to be overhauled. The system might be improved by including higher taxes on packaging, banning certain unrecyclable plastics and throwaway products, and instituting standards for making products last longer. In addition, industries need assurances that the supply of recyclable materials is abundant and reliable. Tax breaks might encourage industries to use recyclable materials. Manufacturers should be discouraged from making durable goods that do not last or that waste energy, and encouraged to use recycled materials whenever possible. These steps could be taken without requiring major changes in our lifestyle, while vastly improving the environment.

ALTERNATIVE FORMS OF ENERGY

An energy crisis of immense proportions looms ahead if alternative sources of energy are not found and exploited before petroleum begins to run out. Nuclear energy is one of the best solutions to the world's chronic energy problems. Many European countries, particularly France, rely heavily on nuclear energy to replace costly fossil fuels. To combat atmospheric pollution and global climate change, a reassessment of nuclear energy is needed, because nuclear electrical generating plants are essentially nonpolluting. However, the safety of the plants must be ensured and nuclear wastes have to be managed properly (Fig. 5-11) if nuclear energy is to be considered a viable alternative energy source.

Figure 5–11 An underground nuclear waste disposal site in a salt bed 2,000 feet below the surface near Carlsbad, New Mexico. Courtesy of U.S. Department of Energy

Much research has been done on fusion energy (Fig. 5-12) because it is both renewable and essentially nonpolluting. Fusion is safe, and its byproducts are energy and helium, a harmless gas that escapes into space. Many advances in fusion research have been made, but a workable electrical generating station using fusion is still many decades away. Unless a major breakthrough is made soon and the technology is rapidly commercialized, fusion would not figure significantly as an energy source in the near future.

Another successful energy alternative is solar energy. The sun is a colossal nuclear reactor that radiates a tremendous amount of energy. The sunlight striking the Earth is equivalent to about 15,000 times the world's present energy supply. Photovoltaic, or solar, cells can convert sunlight directly into electricity, with an optimum efficiency of about 20 percent. The manufacture of solar cells is very expensive, however, making large-scale use uneconomical. But less efficient solar cells can be manufactured in mass quantities at greatly reduced prices.

A more successful means of converting sunlight into electricity are vast arrays of solar collectors combined in solar farms (Fig. 5-13). Sunlight is

ITER

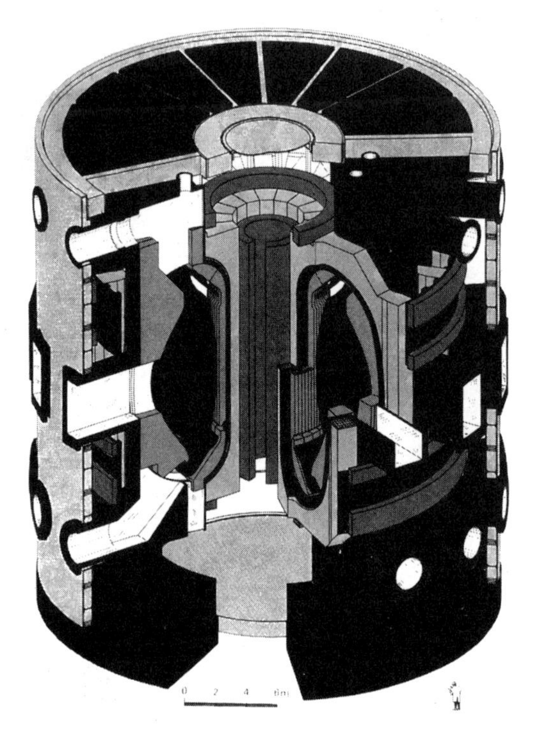

Figure 5–12 An artist's rendition of the International Fusion Experiment (ITER) at Princeton, New Jersey. Courtesy of U.S. Department of Energy

focused into a powerful narrow beam by banks of heliostatic mirrors that automatically track the sun as it travels across the sky. The light beam is directed onto a central receiving station, where the intensified light heats a boiler and superheated steam drives a turbine generator. At present, however, solar power stations cannot compete economically with conventional fossil fuel generating plants. But this could change as fossil fuels become scarce and expensive.

Commercial and residential buildings can utilize solar energy to supplement conventional water heaters and furnaces. This conversion can provide substantial savings on utility bills, while conserving nonrenewable energy resources. The Sun Belt states of the Southwest, which receive a

Figure 5–13 An artist's rendition of a solar electrical generation station. Courtesy of U.S. Department of Energy

Figure 5–14a A wind-powered electrical generation station, near Livermore, California. Courtesy of U.S. Department of Energy

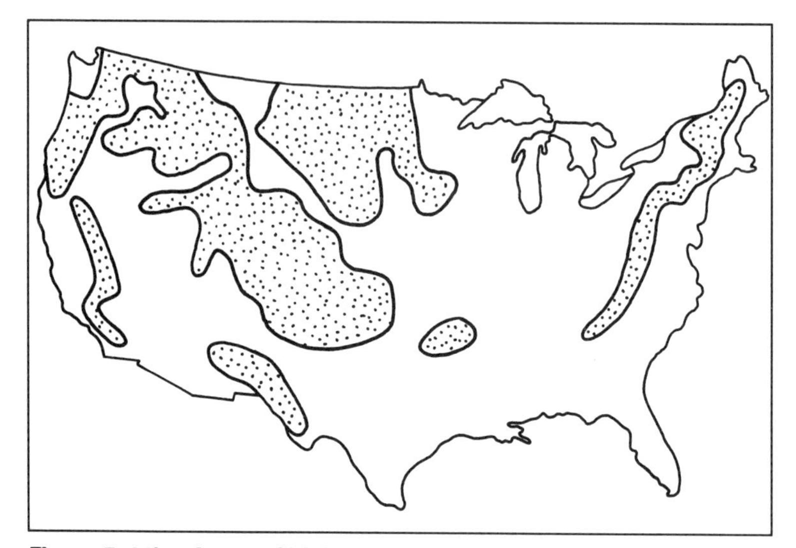

Figure 5–14b Areas of high wind velocity in the United States.

generous supply of sunlight, can take full advantage of this type of solar energy. The systems usually pay for themselves in utilities savings in about a decade.

In windy localities, such as seacoasts, where the offshore and onshore wind currents are reliable, utilities construct large windmills to generate electricity (Figs. 5-14 a&b). About 90 percent of the U.S. wind power potential lies in 12 north-central and western states. The wind also drives ocean waves, which could be harnessed to produce electricity. Trapping tidewaters in enclosed bays is a means of generating electricity from the power of falling water. Another important use of falling water is hydroelectric dams. However, hydroelectric projects are expensive, and the most accessible sites have either been exploited or deemed unacceptable due to the necessary flooding of large tracts of valuable land.

A little-known energy source is ocean thermal-energy conversion, or OTEC. It takes advantage of the temperature difference between thermal layers of the ocean to generate electricity by utilizing a large, low-pressure steam generator. The plants also produce fresh water as a by-product,—another valuable resource. Many coastal areas around the world can take advantage of this unique form of solar energy.

The potential for geothermal energy is enormous, and that of the U.S. alone is about 10 times the heat energy of all its coal deposits. Many steam and geyser fields are associated with active volcanism, which makes these areas ideal sites for tapping geothermal energy for steam heat and electrical power generation. In other areas without natural geysers, geothermal energy can be extracted from fractured, hot, dry rock, in a method whereby water is injected into deep wells and steam is recovered. Unfortunately, overproduction of steam fields such as The Geysers in California (Fig. 5-15), the largest geothermal electrical generating plant in the world, could rapidly deplete this valuable natural resource.

The geopressured energy deposits beneath the Gulf Coast off Texas and Louisiana are a hybrid of geothermal energy and fossil fuel in reservoirs of hot gas-charged seawater. The deposits were formed millions of years ago when seawater was trapped in porous beds of sandstone between impermeable clay layers. Heat building up from below was captured in the seawater along with methane from decaying organic matter. As more

Figure 5–15 A geothermal generating plant at The Geysers near San Francisco, California. Courtesy of U.S. Department of Energy

Figure 5–16 A drilling rig extracts geopressured energy near Houston, Texas.
Courtesy of U.S. Department of Energy

sediments piled on, the hot gas-charged seawater became highly pressurized. Wells drilled into this formation (Fig. 5-16) not only tap geothermal energy but also natural gas, providing an energy potential equal to about one-third that of all coal deposits in the United States.

6

CLIMATE CHANGE

Human activities responsible for changing the gaseous composition of the atmosphere threaten to produce global climate change over the next several decades. Increasing amounts of atmospheric carbon dioxide (Fig. 6-1), along with other man-made greenhouse gases, principally methane, not only tend to warm the planet but could energize the atmosphere and alter the hydrologic cycle, which is responsible for bringing rain to all parts of the world.

The rise in global temperatures also could cause part of the polar ice caps to melt and raise sea levels, flooding the coastal regions where half the world's population lives. Shifting precipitation patterns could cause serious drought and desertification in some regions and severe flooding in others, thus dramatically reducing agricultural output. Changing atmospheric circulation patterns could significantly affect the weather, resulting in a larger number of violent storms, and potentially much death and destruction.

CLIMATES FOR HUMANITY

Several hundred million years ago, when forests first spanned the continents (Fig. 6-2), the global environment was quite different from what it is today; the climate of those times would have been quite inhospitable to human beings. During the past few million years, and especially during the

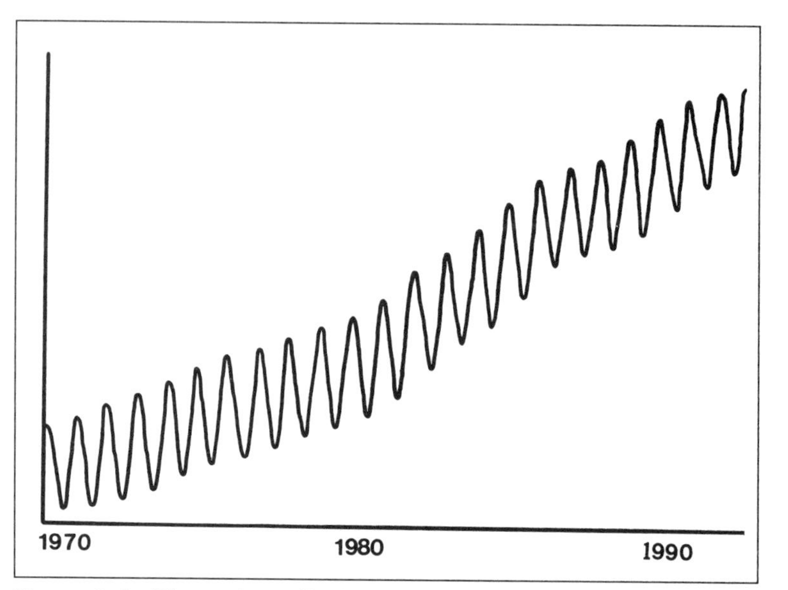

Figure 6–1 **The carbon dioxide concentration in the atmosphere varies with the seasons and increases with time.**

Figure 6–2 **Fossilized tree trunks at Petrified Forest National Monument, Apache County, Arizona.** Photo by Darton, courtesy of USGS

last 8,000 years, the Earth's climate has been extremely beneficial to humankind, and people have prospered exceedingly under these benign conditions. Now it appears that the climate is changing again—possibly to one much less to our liking.

One of the most dramatic climate changes in the history of the planet occurred during our present interglacial, called the Holocene epoch, which coincides with the rise of civilization. When the glaciers departed at the end of the last ice age, Africa and Arabia, which were tropical regions at that time, began to dry out. The climate change caused by the rapid warming resulted in the expansion of the arid regions between 14,000 and 12,500 years ago.

During a wet period, from 12,000 to 6,000 years ago, some of today's African deserts were covered with lush vegetation and contained numerous large lakes. Lake Chad on the southern border of the Sahara Desert was Africa's largest lake; its area was 10 times its present size. Lakes in other parts of the world were similarly affected. Utah's Great Salt Lake occupied the adjacent salt flats, expanding to several times its current size.

Following the retreating glaciers of the last ice age, plants and animals returned to the northern latitudes. The long wet spell might have been caused by the strengthening of the monsoons, which carry moisture-laden sea breezes inland over Africa, India, and southeast Asia. The continental interiors 9,000 years ago were warmer in summer, which invigorated the monsoon winds. The Climatic Optimum, which began about 6,000 years ago, was a period of unusually warm, wet conditions that lasted for 2,000 years, during which time early civilizations prospered.

About 4,000 years ago, temperatures dropped significantly and the world became drier, forming today's deserts. Around 1,000 years ago, the world warmed again, during the Medieval Climate Maximum. Some 500 years later, the world plunged into the Little Ice Age, which lasted three centuries and caused average global temperatures to drop about 1 degree Celsius (2 degrees Fahrenheit). The expanding glaciers forced people out of the northlands of Europe and decimated the Greenland Normans, who had successfully inhabited the island for nearly 500 years. By the middle 19th century, the world began to warm again until 1938, cooled until 1976, and presently appears to be in another long-term warming trend that shows no signs of abating.

GLOBAL WARMING

Major climate changes are taking place, and apparently our species is responsible for some of the climatic disturbances that beset our planet. By the middle of the next century, the Earth could become warmer than at any

TABLE 6–1 MAJOR DESERTS OF THE WORLD

Desert	Location	Type	Area in Square Miles (in thousands)
Sahara	North Africa	Tropical	3,500
Australian	Western/interior	Tropical	1,300
Arabian	Arabian Peninsula	Tropical	1,000
Turkestan	S. Central Asia	Continental	750
North American	Southwestern U.S./Northern Mexico	Continental	500
Patagonian	Argentina	Continental	260
Thar	India/Pakastan	Tropical	230
Kalahari	Southwestern Africa	Littoral	220
Gobi	Mongolia/China	Continental	200
Takla Makan	Sinkiang, China	Continental	200
Iranian	Iran/Afganistan	Tropical	150
Atacama	Peru/Chile	Littoral	140

time during the past million years if we do not curb our insatiable appetite for fossil fuels and cease the widespread destruction of forests and other wildlife habitats. These climate changes likely result from high-level emissions of carbon dioxide, amounting to over 7 billion tons per year, along with other man-made greenhouse gases. Some of these artificial gases are extremely toxic and carcinogenic, and appear to be capable of causing higher cancer rates. Other man-made substances are apparently destroying the ozone layer, without which life could not exist on the surface of the Earth.

Over the last decade, record-breaking weather events have occurred worldwide. In the United States, the 1980s witnessed six of the seven hottest years since the end of the Little Ice Age 140 years ago, even surpassing the Dust Bowl years of the 1930s, the country's greatest ecological disaster of the century (Fig. 6-3). The remainder of this century promises continued warming. These events could be symptoms of a global climate change resulting from the chemical pollution of the atmosphere.

The strange weather could just be a reflection of natural climate variability (Fig. 6-4). So far, no clear sign of climate change has appeared that positively can be blamed on greenhouse warming. Unknown moderating factors could cancel out part of the greenhouse effect. Even man-made

Figure 6–3 The 1936 Dust Bowl in Cimarron County, Oklahoma. Photo by A. Rothstein, courtesy of USDA–Soil Conservation Service

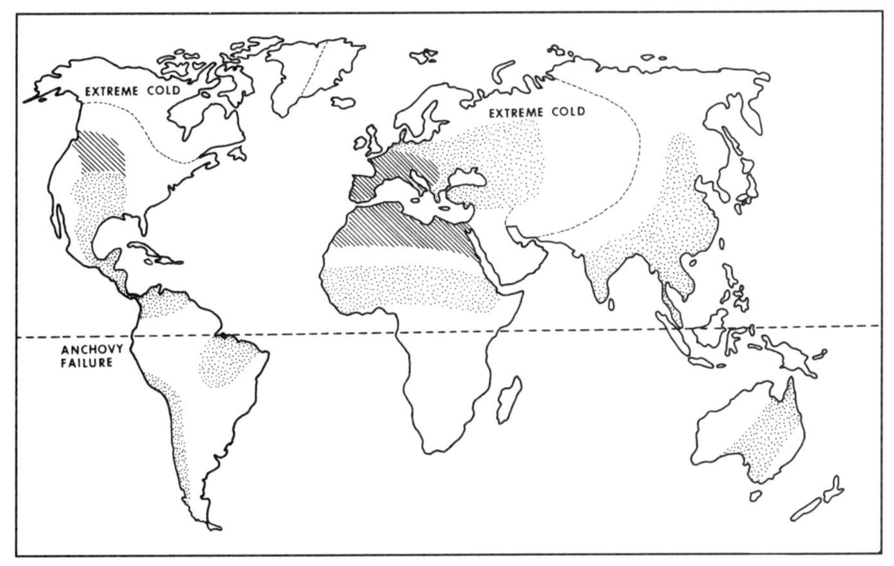

Figure 6–4 Strange weather of 1972. Stippled areas were affected by extreme drought, hash marked areas by unusually wet weather. This El Niño event destroyed much of the anchovy catch off the coast of Peru.

pollutant aerosols or massive volcanism like the June 1991 eruption of the Philippine volcano Pinatubo, possibly the largest blast of the century, might slow greenhouse warming by reflecting sunlight back into space. Instruments aboard the Earth Radiation Budget Satellite detected a nearly 4 percent increase in sunlight reflected by the atmosphere months after the eruption, reducing average global temperatures by at least 0.5 degrees Celsius.

While volcanic ash falls out of the atmosphere rather quickly, in a matter of weeks or months, volcanic aerosols, chiefly sulfur dioxide, linger for up to three years or more. During the past 100 years, the global temperature has dropped several tenths of a degree within one to two years following large volcanic eruptions. Perhaps greenhouse warming will become more obvious in the next few years once the climate system recovers from recent volcanic eruptions.

Climatologists do not fully comprehend the intricate mechanisms involved in greenhouse warming. However, the results of a steady rise in atmospheric carbon dioxide probably would be catastrophic if other moderating factors did not come into play. These might include the absorption of excess carbon dioxide and heat by the oceans and green vegetation on land. Most of the carbon that flows through the ocean is in the form of organic debris produced by plants and animals. But these processes act largely to transfer carbon from shallow waters to the abyss, and do little to draw carbon dioxide out of the atmosphere. Furthermore, warmer sea temperatures reduce the ocean's ability to absorb excess carbon dioxide and could even increase the expulsion of the gas, as does warming a bottle of soda.

Where all the carbon dioxide produced by industrial activities is going remains a mystery. Apparently only about 40 percent of the carbon dioxide generated by the combustion of fossil fuels and the destruction of forests is accumulating in the atmosphere and being absorbed by the ocean. Some excess carbon dioxide might be absorbed by terrestrial vegetation, acting like a fertilizer to stimulate plant growth. Nevertheless, land plants do not store as much carbon dioxide as the oceans and might reach full capacity in the foreseeable future. Furthermore, the continuing destruction of the world's forests dramatically reduces their ability to absorb excess carbon dioxide.

Possibly within 50 to 100 years, the world could become hotter than it was 3 million years ago, prior to the onset of the Pleistocene glaciation. The temperature rise would result from high levels of atmospheric carbon dioxide, which account for almost 60 percent of the annual human contribution of greenhouse gases. The greatest rise in temperature would occur at the higher latitudes of the Northern Hemisphere, with the largest increases during winter.

Figure 6–5 The Anaktuvuk district, Northern Alaska, showing polygonal markings on the ground surface. Photo by Fellows, courtesy of USGS

One horrifying aspect of global warming would be the thawing of the arctic tundra (Fig. 6-5), releasing into the atmosphere vast quantities of carbon dioxide and methane trapped in the soil, possibly causing a runaway greenhouse effect. Evidence collected from Alaska's northern tundra suggests that global warming might already be spurring the release of carbon dioxide from the land. A combination of methane and water ice forms a clathrate (a cell-like chemical mixture) in the bottom muds of the deep sea, and ocean warming could expel massive quantities of methane into the atmosphere, which along with carbon dioxide could create a vicious cycle of heat and release.

The buildup of atmospheric methane also stems from a population explosion of termites, from deforestation and from increasing numbers of rice fields and domestic animals, which constitute an even larger source. Furthermore, methane remains in the atmosphere much longer than carbon dioxide, persisting for a decade or more.

The present warming trend amounts to an increase of about 0.5 degrees Celsius during this century. Since about 1850, when the world thawed out following the Little Ice Age, global temperatures have steadily increased (Fig. 6-6). The rising temperature trend was briefly interrupted by a cooling spell between 1940 and 1976 resulting from an increase in volcanic activity. Since then, temperatures have resumed their upward rise. Meanwhile, the carbon dioxide content of the atmosphere has increased more than 20 percent over this century and could double by the middle of the next

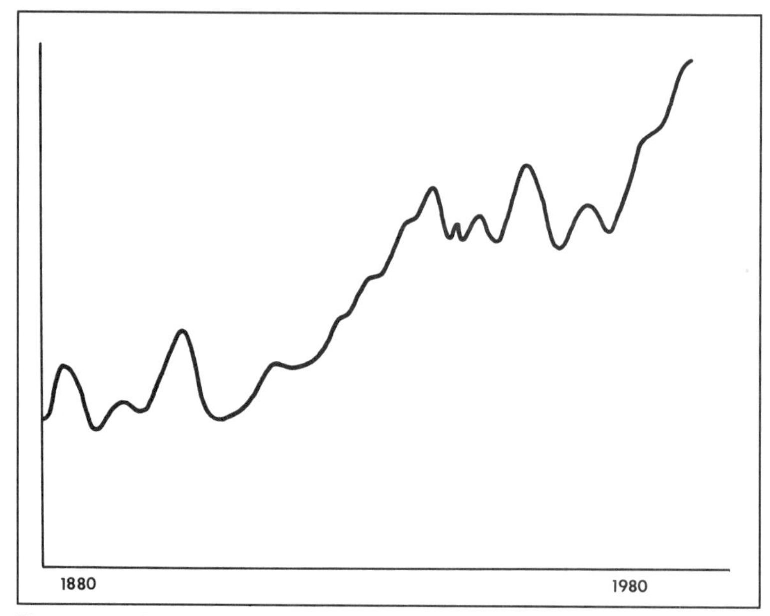

Figure 6–6 The rise in global temperatures during the last hundred years.

Figure 6–7 A forest fire engulfed half of Yellowstone National Park in the summer and fall of 1988. Courtesy of National Park Service

century, possibly raising average global temperatures 1.5 to 4.5 degrees Celsius, creating some of the warmest temperatures since the days of the dinosaurs.

The most unusual aspect of the present global warming trend is its unprecedented speed. The temperature rise is 10 to 20 times faster than the average rate of warming after the last ice age. Between 14,000 and 10,000 years ago, when massive ice sheets across North America and Eurasia melted, the Earth warmed perhaps 3 to 5 degrees Celsius, comparable to the predicted increase for global warming. The major difference, however, is that the temperature increase extended over a period of several thousand years and was not compressed into a mere century.

By the end of the next century, global temperatures could equal those of 100 million years ago during one of the warmest periods in geologic history. If that happened, some areas in the Northern Hemisphere would dry out, creating a large potential for massive forest fires. This has dire implications, because if greenhouse warming continues, major forest fires like those that devastated half of Yellowstone National Park in 1988 (Fig. 6-7) might become more frequent, with substantial losses of forests and wildlife habitats.

Increasing surface temperatures, like those experienced as a result of El Niño, the warm inshore current flowing from Central America, could have an adverse effect on global precipitation patterns (Fig. 6-8). Subtropical regions might experience a marked decrease in precipitation, encouraging the spread of deserts. Increasing the area of desert and semidesert regions

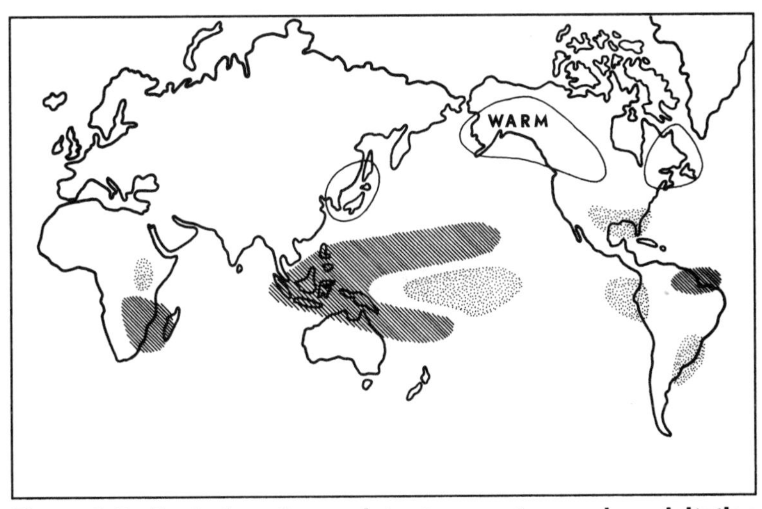

Figure 6-8 Typical northern winter temperature and precipitation patterns during El Niño warming in the central Pacific. Hash marked areas are dry; stippled areas are wet; and encircled areas are warm.

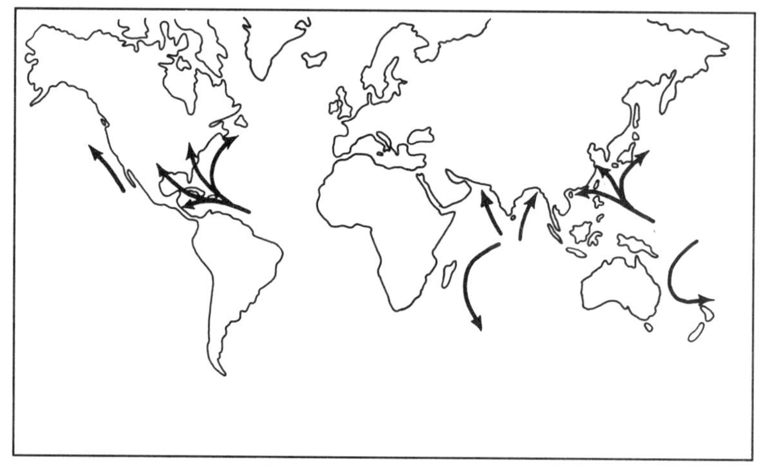

Figure 6–9 Typical paths taken by hurricanes.

would significantly affect agriculture, which would migrate to higher latitudes. Canada and Russia might then become breadbaskets, while the United States would be forced to import grain. Unfortunately, the soils in the northern regions are thin because of glacial erosion and would be quickly depleted by extensive agriculture.

Changes in precipitation patterns would also have profound effects on the distribution of water resources needed for irrigation. Higher temperatures would augment evaporation and diminish the flow of some rivers by 50 percent or more, while other streams could dry out entirely. During the 1988 drought, the Mississippi River fell to a record low, making navigation impossible over long stretches, and allowing ancient sunken wrecks to became visible for the first time in this century. Major groundwater supplies also would be adversely affected, as water tables drop and wells go dry.

Other areas could receive a marked increase in precipitation, causing extensive flooding. Greenhouse warming would energize the atmosphere, making storm systems increasingly more violent. Moreover, changing weather patterns caused by instabilities in the atmosphere could create deserts out of once-productive farmlands, while drenching other regions and causing severe floods and soil erosion. Larger-than-normal seasonal temperature variations might occur, along with a higher atmospheric moisture content, producing storms of unprecedented proportions.

The central regions of the continents, which normally experience occasional droughts, would become permanently dry wastelands. The soils in almost all of Europe, Asia, and North America would dry out, requiring upwards of 50 percent more irrigation. Expected rises in temperatures, increased evaporation, and changes in rainfall patterns would severely limit the export of excess food to developing nations during times of famine. Dry winds of tornadic force would create gigantic dust storms and severe erosional problems. Tornadoes, hailstorms, thunderstorms, and lightning storms would increase in frequency and intensity. Numerous immense hurricanes would charge headlong into heavily populated coastal areas (Fig. 6-9), resulting in tremendous property damage and great loss of life.

RISING SEA LEVELS

As global temperatures increase, coastal regions where half the people of the world live would feel the adverse effects of rising sea levels resulting from melting ice caps and thermal expansion of the ocean. The additional fresh water in the North Atlantic could affect the flow of the Gulf Stream, causing Europe to freeze while the rest of the world heats.

If the present melting continues, the sea could rise a foot or more by the year 2030. For every foot of sea level rise, 100 to 1,000 feet of shoreline is

Figure 6–10 Old stumps and roots exposed by shore erosion at Dewey Beach, Delaware indicate that this area was once the tree zone. Photo by J. Bister, courtesy of USDA–Soil Conservation Service

inundated (Fig. 6-10), depending on the slope of the coast. The receding shoreline would result in the loss of large tracts of coastal land along with shallow barrier islands. Low-lying fertile deltas that support millions of people would disappear. Delicate wetlands, where many species of marine life hatch their young, would vanish. Vulnerable coastal cities would have to rebuild farther inland or construct protective seawalls to hold back the ocean.

Steep waves that accompany storms at sea cause serious erosion (Fig. 6-11). The constant pounding of the surf also erodes most man-made defenses against the rising sea. Upwards of 90 percent of America's once-sandy beaches are sinking beneath the waves. Barrier islands and sandbars running along the East Coast and the Gulf Coast of Texas are disappearing at alarming rates. Sea cliffs are eroding back several feet a year. In Califor-

Figure 6–11 Property damage during a storm at Kitty Hawk, North Carolina. Photo by R. Dolan, courtesy of USGS

Figure 6–12 Chickamin Glacier on the eastern slopes of Dome Peak, Glacier Peak Wilderness, Skagit County, Washington. Photo by Austin Post, courtesy of USGS

nia, huge chunks of land fall into the sea, often destroying expensive homes. Most defenses for halting beach erosion eventually fail, as waves relentlessly batter the coastline.

The sea level is rising up to 10 times faster than it did during the middle of this century, amounting to about a quarter inch per year. Most of the increase appears to result from melting ice caps, particularly in West Antarctica and Greenland. More icebergs are calving off glaciers entering the sea, and they appear to be getting larger as well, threatening the stability of the ice sheets. Alpine glaciers, which contain substantial quantities of ice (Fig. 6-12), are melting as well, possibly due to a warmer climate.

To determine whether greenhouse gases are actually warming the planet, scientists are studying the speed at which sound waves travel through the ocean. Since sound travels faster in warm water than in cold water—a phenomenon known as acoustic thermometry—a decade of measurements could reveal whether global warming is a certainty. The idea is to send out low-frequency sound waves from a single station and monitor them from several listening posts scattered around the world. The signals take several hours to reach the most distant stations. Therefore, shaving a few seconds

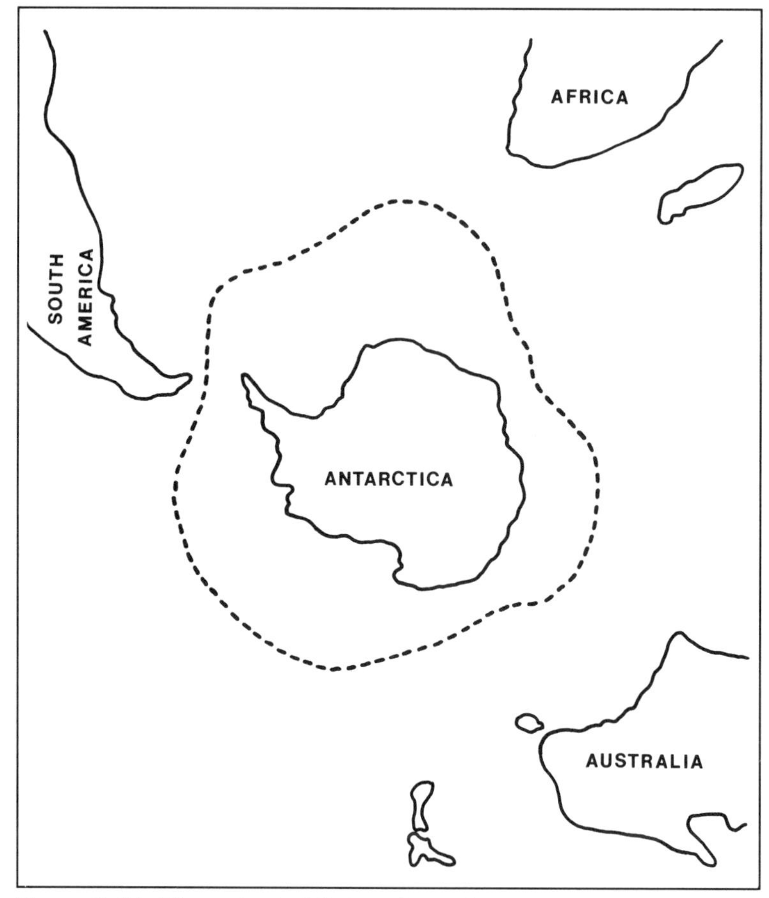

Figure 6–13 The extent of Antarctic sea ice.

off the travel time over an extended period of 5 to 10 years could indicate that the oceans are indeed warming.

The first direct measurements of a possible ocean warming from rising global temperatures were taken by satellites. The polar sea ice appears to have shrunk by as much as 6 percent during the decades of the 1970s and 1980s. However, an extensive study of temperatures over the Arctic Ocean indicates that the region has not warmed significantly over the last four decades. Perhaps the Arctic is the last region affected by greenhouse warming. Sea ice covers most of the Arctic Ocean and forms a frozen band around Antarctica (Fig. 6-13) during the winter season in each hemisphere. If global warming melts the polar sea ice, the number of microscopic organisms could fall, along with the populations of marine animals that feed on them.

DROUGHT AND DESERTIFICATION

The increase in global temperatures could dramatically affect the climate by shifting precipitation patterns throughout the world, bringing unusually wet conditions to some regions and drought to others. Greenhouse warming is also likely to increase both the frequency and severity of droughts.

The measure of tree rings (Fig. 6-14) provides an indicator of past climates: generally speaking, the wider the rings the more favorable the climate. During droughts or cold periods, tree rings are usually narrower because of poor growing conditions. Analysis of tree rings of the bristlecone pine, among the longest-living plants on Earth, provides a drought index for the western United States dating back to the year A.D. 1600. Tree rings of ancient, well-preserved trees can tell of a region's climate history going back more than 7,000 years.

Droughts result from shifting of precipitation activities around the world. Since the Earth's total heat budget does not change significantly from one year to the next, areas that become unusually dry are matched, to some extent, by areas that become exceptionally wet. For example, during the

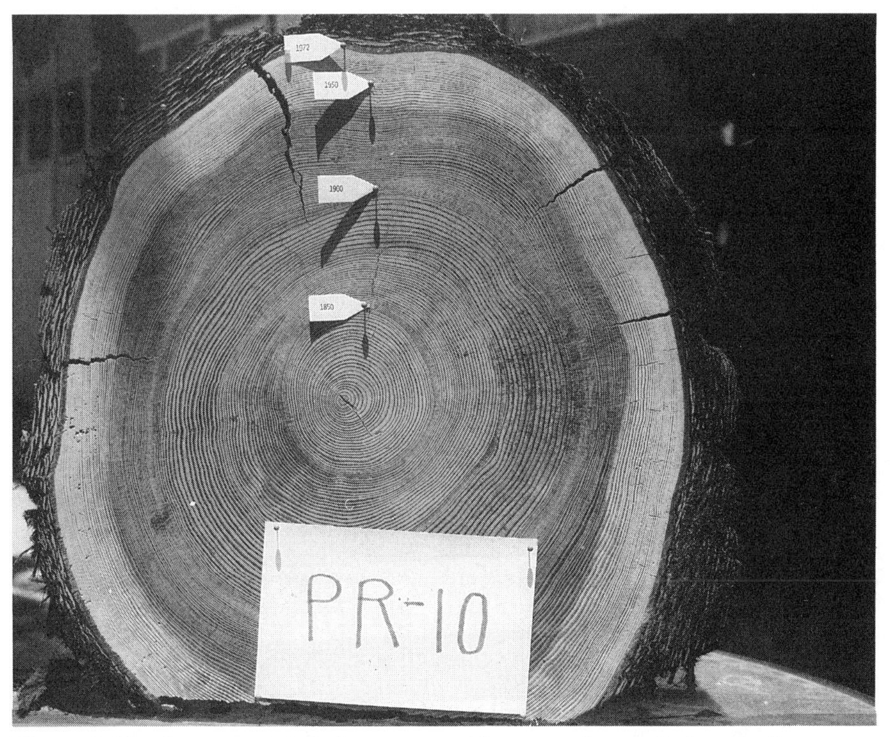

Figure 6–14 A tree sample being prepared for annual growth ring studies. Photo by L. E. Jackson, courtesy of USGS

decade of the 1980s, the United States endured a series of bad droughts. In 1983, Australia had its most severe drought in over 100 years. An equally intense drought caused food shortages in southern Africa and also affected western Africa and the Sahel south of the Sahara Desert. Meanwhile, the worst flooding of the century struck many parts of South America.

Half the people of the world depend on the monsoon rains for their survival (Fig. 6-15). The monsoons are seasonal changes in wind direction that alternately produce wet summers and dry winters. During the rainy season, drenching squalls lasting a week or so are interspersed with equal periods of sunny weather. During the monsoon's dormant phase, the weather is hot, dry, and stable. If the monsoons do not occur due to climatic disturbances, millions of people are placed in jeopardy. As the world's population continues to grow, a major drought caused by the failure of the monsoon winds could turn into the most horrendous tragedy in human history.

Desertification is a process of environmental degradation that is a product of changing climate and of human activity. It results from the loss of topsoil, which takes millions of acres of agricultural land out of production each year. After the land is stripped of its topsoil, only the coarse sands of the subsoil remain, creating a man-made desert. The problem is exacerbated when the land is subjected to flash floods, higher erosion rates, and dust storms that sweep the sands from place to place.

The process of desertification occurs in all parts of the world, but it is most pervasive in central Africa, where the sands of the Sahara Desert

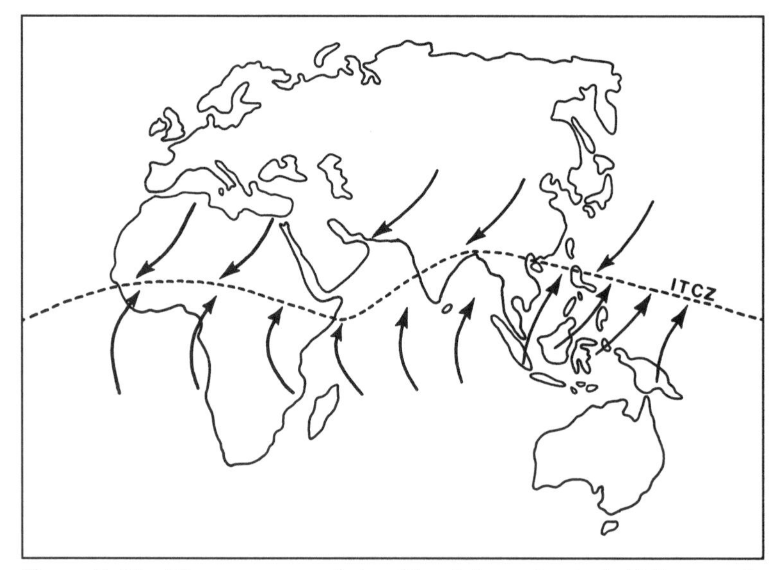

Figure 6–15 The monsoons bring life-giving rains to half the people of the world.

steadily march across once-fertile farmland. Desertification is also self-perpetuating, because the bare ground reflects more sunlight, producing high-pressure regions that block out weather systems and reduce rainfall.

Furthermore, the land is subjected to flash floods and dust storms, which transport the sediments out of the region and deposit them elsewhere. Throughout the world, from one third to one half of once-fertile lands are now rendered useless by erosion and desertification. Even in the United States, half of the arable land could be lost by the middle of the next century.

COMBATING CLIMATE CHANGE

One response strategy for combating climate change would be moving to a cooler climate or building expensive coastal defenses against a rising sea

Figure 6–16 Sea walls along Fenwick Island, Worcester County, Maryland. Photo by R. Dolan, courtesy of USGS

(Fig. 6-16). Another plan might require the limitation or reduction of greenhouse gas emissions. Conservation is the preferred method for combating climate change and would result in large part from improved energy efficiency along with the development of nonpolluting substitute energy sources. The adoption of these measures would also make our world more ecologically sound.

The theory of climate change has so many complex variables that predicting the weather well into the future is extremely difficult. Since the climate has always been changing, even from year to year often bringing weather extremes, any future changes could still result from natural causes. Thus far, no clear sign of greenhouse warming has occurred over this century. Because the present effects of global climate change seem relatively mild, no drastic actions or sacrifices are deemed necessary for the time being. Most scientists and policymakers prefer to wait and see whether or not climate change becomes a reality.

TABLE 6–2 THE WARMEST, WETTEST, AND WINDIEST CITIES IN THE UNITED STATES

Extreme	Location	Average Annual Value
Warmest	Key West, FL	Mean temperature 78 deg. F.
Coldest	International Falls, MN	Mean temperature 36 deg. F.
Sunniest	Yuma, AZ	348 sunny days
Driest	Yuma, AZ	2.7 inches of rainfall
Wettest	Quillayute, WA	105 inches of rainfall
Rainiest	Quillayute, WA	212 rainy days
Cloudiest	Quillayute, WA	242 cloudy days
Snowiest	Blue Canyon, CA	243 inches of snowfall
Windiest	Blue Hill, MA	Mean wind speed 15 mph

More research is needed on atmospheric physics and air–sea interactions, using the most powerful computers to model the data. Much information about the Earth could be collected by advanced space technology (Fig. 6-17). Since the amounts of information amassed will be so huge, a decade or more might be required to analyze the data. Perhaps, if an upward trend in temperature continues into the next century the climate change could definitely be attributed to the greenhouse effect.

However, whether the human race has that much time is uncertain. If we wait too long to put corrective measures in place, much more drastic steps might be required to counter global warming in the future. Furthermore,

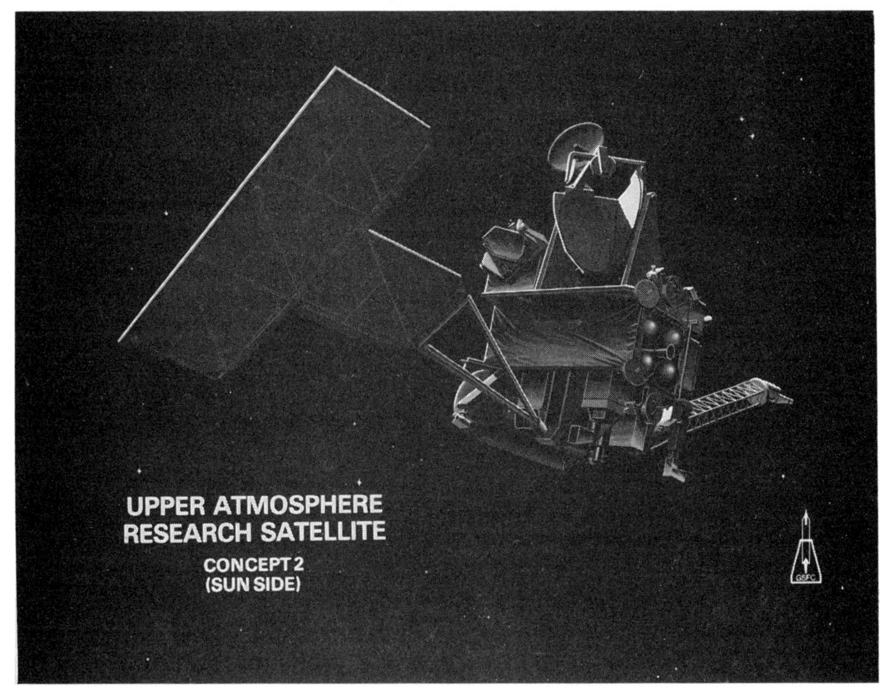

Figure 6–17 The Upper Atmosphere Research Satellite will measure ozone and other constituents in the upper atmosphere. Courtesy of NASA

lead times for building greenhouse-combating projects, such as nuclear or solar electrical power plants, might require a decade or more. The thermal inertia of the ocean could delay the onset of greenhouse warming by several decades, by which time the effects of global warming could be catastrophic.

7

CARRYING CAPACITY

Human beings have long regarded Earth as theirs for the taking, and believed that nature should be tamed for their exclusive benefit. Unfortunately, the environmental consequences of this short-sighted attitude have been profound and highly disruptive. As hunter-gatherers, humans were keenly aware of their environment, its resources, and its dangers. Populations remained fairly stable, and rarely did humans exceed the carrying capacity of their habitat. However, population growth, which previously had been held in check by the harsh demands of the natural world, soared when nature came under the plow.

The present population growth rate, about 1.7 percent per annum, is hundreds of times greater than during most of human history. Overpopulation is causing greater hardships than all the trials humans have ever faced. A deadly combination of drought, disease, and infestation from continued global climate change and the loss of agricultural land and marine fisheries could conspire against humanity, causing the greatest famine and the largest death toll from starvation the world has ever known.

FOOD AND POPULATION

The world is rapidly approaching, if not already exceeding, its carrying capacity—the ability of the land to support human populations. A popula-

Figure 7–1 An open pit copper mine, Greenlee County, Arizona. Mineral and energy depletion effects a nation's carrying capacity. Courtesy of USGS

tion surpasses its carrying capacity when it can no longer be maintained without the rapid depletion of natural resources including energy and minerals (Fig. 7-1). However, the most important resource is food, and a nation that cannot adequately feed itself is therefore overpopulated. By that definition, most developing countries of the world are overpopulated as are many developed nations. Russia, for example, frequently experiences crop shortages and must import food.

About 3.5 billion people worldwide live in poverty, and one-fifth of the human race lives in abject destitution. Several heavily populated nations have difficulty feeding, clothing, sheltering, and employing their people at more than a subsistence level.

Rapid population growth has stretched the resources of the world, and the prospect of future increases raises serious doubts whether the planet can continue to support people's growing needs: A shortage in petroleum would result in a shortage of nitrogen-based fertilizers, as well as fuel for pumping the world's irrigation water. The developing countries with the highest birthrates and with falling death rates find that economic gains are quickly eroded simply by having too many additional mouths to feed.

The developing nations of Asia, Africa, and South America are in a desperate race to keep food supplies in step with population growth. The countries of sub-Saharan Africa have a total population of about 500 million people, a figure that could double in just two decades. About 100 million Africans are seriously malnourished, and a quarter of the children born there die before the age of five. During the last two decades, millions of people have died of famine and hunger-related causes. When drought and famine strike in these regions, there is grave danger of mass starvation, especially if for political or other reasons food imports cannot meet the demand, as in Somalia.

About 90 percent of the world's food is supplied by only a dozen crops, and half the human population relies on rice as its main staple. The majority of crop strains are genetically undiversified. For example, most corn grown in the United States is planted with descendants of only six inbred varieties. With the continued destruction of the world's rain forests and the extinction of valuable plant species, the human race is rapidly losing the ability to develop new strains of agricultural crops that have special defenses against a variety of attacks that reduce crop yields. Without the diversification of agricultural

Figure 7–2 Hail damage can severely reduce crop yields. Courtesy of NOAA

Figure 7–3 The United States has most of its arable land in production, as shown here by these loess uplands abutting farmland near Wauneta, Nebraska.
Photo by W. D. E. Cardwell, courtesy of USGS

crops, disease and infestation targeted at the few specific strains presently available could wipe out a nation's entire harvest.

When agriculture can no longer supply the necessary food, famine inevitably strikes because during periods with favorable climates, when crop yeilds are barely adequate, populations tend to grow well beyond the limits imposed by inevitably unfavorable growing conditions, when harvests are poor. Mass starvation could result from severely reduced crop yields produced by drought, infestation, disease, frost, or storm damage (Fig. 7-2).

The world's leading food exporters already have most of their arable land in production (Fig. 7-3). To increase exports during the 1970s, American farmers put into production an additional 60 million acres—an area larger than the state of Kansas. Much of this acreage was substandard; it included sloping, marginal, and fragile soils that are vulnerable to erosion. As a result, the United States has actually lost agricultural land over the past several years. Also, expanding urbanization removes another million acres of valuable cropland every year.

Under increasing pressure for more food production, normally fallow fields are cultivated, a process that quickly wears out the soil. The United States no longer has an excess capacity in such basic agricultural resources as land, water, and energy. Efforts to farm the weak soils of the rain forests have been disastrous. Overirrigation is destroying large acreages through soil oversalinization on poorly drained fields that do not receive adequate

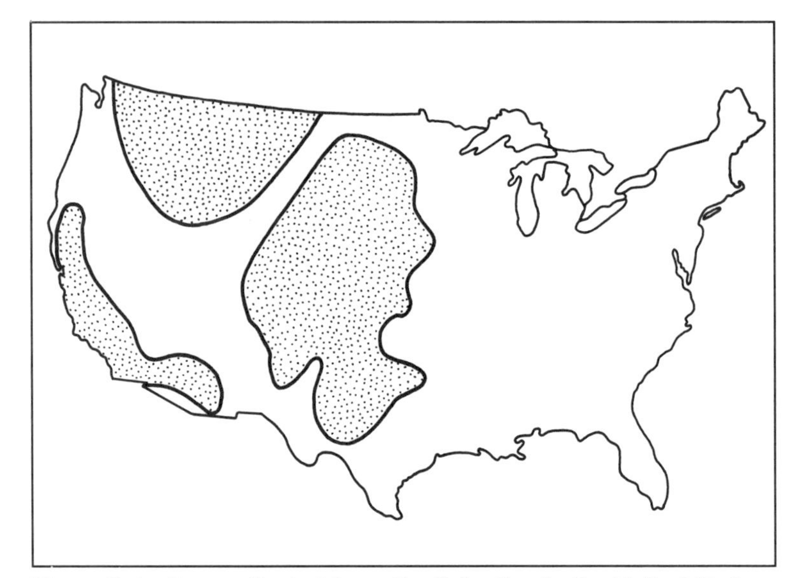

Figure 7–4 Areas affected by soil salinization in the United States

rainfall to flush out salt (Fig. 7-4), which is one of the greatest factors limiting agricultural productivity. (Generally, irrigation water has a high salt content.)

The total amount of food directly and indirectly consumed by the human race is roughly a ton per person per year, or some 5 billion tons annually. Nearly half the total tonnage of crops and three-quarters of the energy and protein content is supplied by cereal grains such as rice, wheat, and barley (Fig. 7-5). However, a large fraction of these grains is fed to domestic animals, which consume 4 to 7 grain calories for every calorie of meat they produce. In addition, pets and sacred animals eat a substantial amount of food. Since about a third of the calories consumed by the developed nations is supplied by animal products, a conversion to a largely vegetarian diet would free additional grain to feed the world's hungry (besides being more healthful).

The average individual food intake among developed nations is about 2,700 calories per day, or about 1,000 more calories than in developing countries. If the actual amount of edible plant products is factored in, including grain for animal feed, Americans consume close to 10,000 calories per person per day. In addition to the much lower calorie count, the diets of citizens of the poorer countries are not as nutritious as those of the richer nations. The diets of the poorest 20 percent of the world's population consist mostly of cereal grains, tubers, and other starchy roots, which together do not supply the body's minimum requirements for a normally active, healthy life.

Figure 7–5 Barley that is about two weeks from harvesting, Howard County, Maryland. Photo by T. McCabe, courtesy of USDA–Soil Conservation Service

DEPLETED FISHERIES

The world's oceans are suffering from a dangerous decline in vitality. The drop in the number of marine animals is too large to be explained by chemical pollution alone, however. Much of the decrease stems from

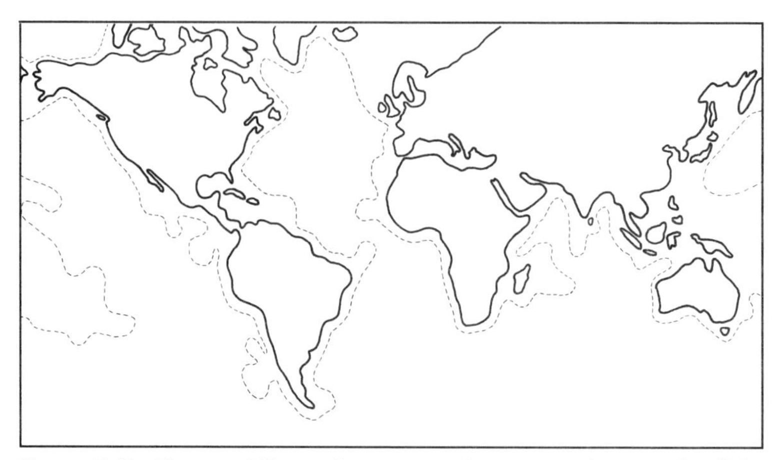

Figure 7–6 The world's marine economic zones, where major fisheries supply human dietary needs.

destructive activities such as dynamite fishing, harvesting fish in spawning grounds, fishing with fine mesh nets that trap immature fish and other species such as dolphins, diverting rivers, and destroying wetlands. If the current practice of exploiting the oceans for short-term gains is not changed, the human race faces a long-term catastrophe, likely culminating with the collapse of the world's fisheries.

A variety of examples among the world's fisheries (Fig. 7-6) show that major fish supplies have collapsed from overfishing. The relative abundance of various species has changed dramatically in many parts of the world. As a result of the constant harvest of a dwindling resource and fluctuating environmental conditions, there has been a major decline in the catch of "good" fish compared to "trash" fish, which are less desirable species. The composition of the catch is also changing toward smaller fish species, and even the average size of fish within the same species is smaller. Thus, previously good fish are now regarded as trash fish because only small individuals are caught.

Overfishing drives populations below the levels needed for competition to regulate the population density of desired species. Therefore, under heavy exploitation, species that can produce offspring quickly and copiously are given a relative advantage—another factor that causes fleshy "good" fish to be replaced by coarser "trash" fish. To what extent these changes are due to shifts in fish populations, changes in patterns of commercial fishing, or environmental effects is uncertain. What is apparent is that if present trends continue, the world's fish supply could become smaller and composed of an increasing percentage of trash fish.

The world's annual fish catch amounts to about 100 million tons, with the northwest Pacific and the northeast Atlantic yielding nearly half the

Figure 7–7 Catfish harvesting on a pond near Tunica, Mississippi.
Photo by D. Warren, courtesy of USDA

total. A pronounced decline in heavily exploited herring and mackerel is compensated for by increased yields of cod, haddock, pollock, and whiting along with other small fishes. To compensate for the loss of marine species, the development of aquaculture at inland fish farms and mariculture, the commercial raising of marine species, can help meet the world's growing demand for fish (Fig. 7-7).

The systematic removal of large predator fish might increase annual catches of other fish by several million tons. But such catches would consist of smaller trash fish that would eventually dominate the northern latitudes, where changes in fish populations tend to be more variable and unpredictable than in the tropical regions. These changes are due to the strongly seasonal behavioral pattern of the fishes as well as to significant differences in climate and other environmental conditions from one season to the next.

Climate change has the potential to dramatically influence fisheries by altering ocean surface temperatures, global circulation patterns, upwelling currents, salinity, pH balance, turbulence, storms, and the distribution of sea ice, all of which affect the primary production of the sea (Fig. 7-8). These conditions could cause a shift in species distribution and loss of species diversity and quantity. As sea levels rise due to ocean warming, coastal wetlands where many species hatch their young would disappear. In addition, an increase of ultaviolet radiation as the ozone layer thins could kill some larval forms of fish and shellfish because they occupy the vulnerable surface waters of the ocean.

Sharks, which have existed for the past 400 million years, play a critical role by preying on sick and injured fish and thus helping to keep the ocean healthy. Unfortunately, commercial shark fishing has caused a marked declined in several shark species, including the thresher, mako, and hammerhead. Shark fishing is extremely wasteful, and up to 90 percent of the U.S. commercial catch is discarded. With an infant mortality exceeding

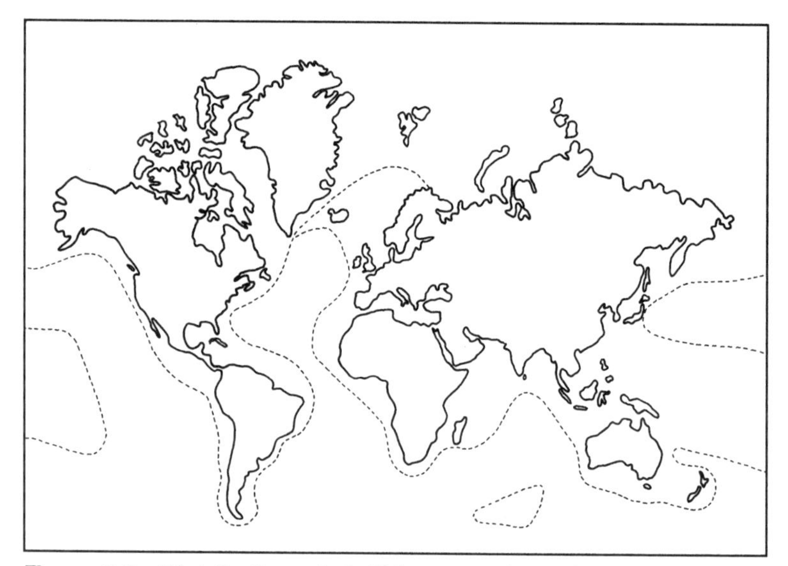

Figure 7–8 Distribution of shelf faunas, where the most valuable fisheries lie.

50 percent, sharks have a difficult time maintaining their numbers. If the present trends continue, many shark species could soon become extinct.

TOPSOIL EROSION

The greatest limiting factor to human population growth is soil erosion (Figs. 7-9 a&b). In about 7000 B.C., the Phoenicians migrated out of the Syrian desert and settled along the eastern Mediterranean coast, where they established the cities of Tyre and Sidon. The land was mountainous and heavily forested with cedars, the primary source of timber for the region. When people had overpopulated the flat plains along the coast, they moved to the slopes, where they cleared and cultivated the upland, severely eroding the soil. Today little is left of the thousand-square-mile forest that once covered the area, and the bare slopes are littered with the remains of ancient terrace walls used in a futile attempt to control erosion.

Figure 7–9a More than 6 billion tons of soil erode from the nation's farmland and other lands each year. Photo by T. McCabe courtesy of USDA–Soil Conservation Service

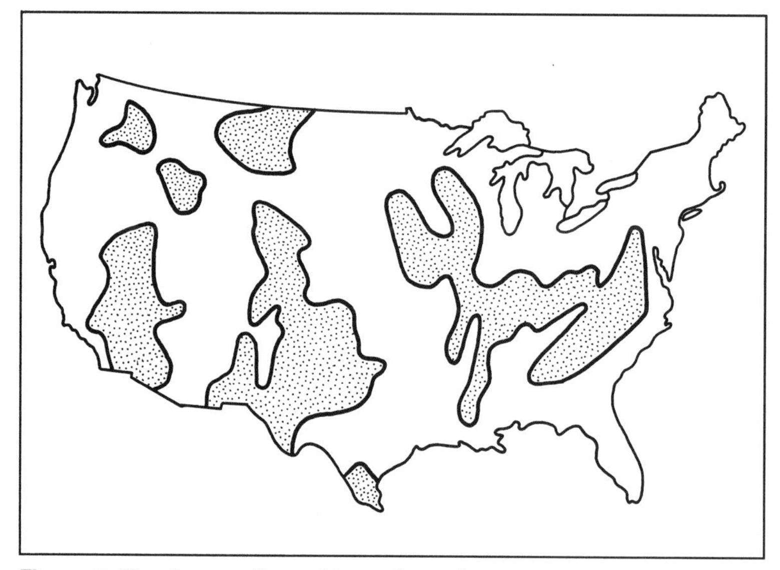

Figure 7–9b Areas affected by soil erosion.

Several once-prosperous cities in northern Syria are now dead. These ancient cities flourished by converting forests into farmland and exporting olive oil and wine. With the invasion of the Persians and Arabs, the collapse of this civilization eliminated all forms of agriculture and up to 6 feet of soil was eroded from the slopes. After 1,300 years of neglect, the once-productive land is now almost completely ravaged, and a man-made desert void of soil, water, and vegetation has taken its place.

Prior to the advent of agriculture about 10,000 years ago, natural soil erosion rates were probably no more than 10 billion tons annually, slow enough for new soil to be generated in its place. However, present soil erosion rates are about 20 billion tons per year, the equivalent of some 15 million acres of arable land. In other words, the world is losing soil twice as fast as nature is putting it back. As much as one-third of the global cropland is losing soil at a rate that is undermining long-term agricultural productivity. World food production per capita could fall substantially if the loss of topsoil continues.

The soil profile (Fig. 7-10) begins with the A zone, which contains most of the soil nutrients. It is a thin bed ranging from a few inches to a few feet in thickness, with an average thickness of 7 inches worldwide. Below this level lies the B zone, which is coarser and of poor soil quality. As the A zone thins and erosion brings the B zone to the surface, the potential for runoff and erosion increases because the poorer soil is generally unsuitable for sustaining vegetation, whose roots hold the soil in place.

Erosion rates vary depending on the amount of precipitation, the topography of the land, the type of rock and soil, and the amount and type of

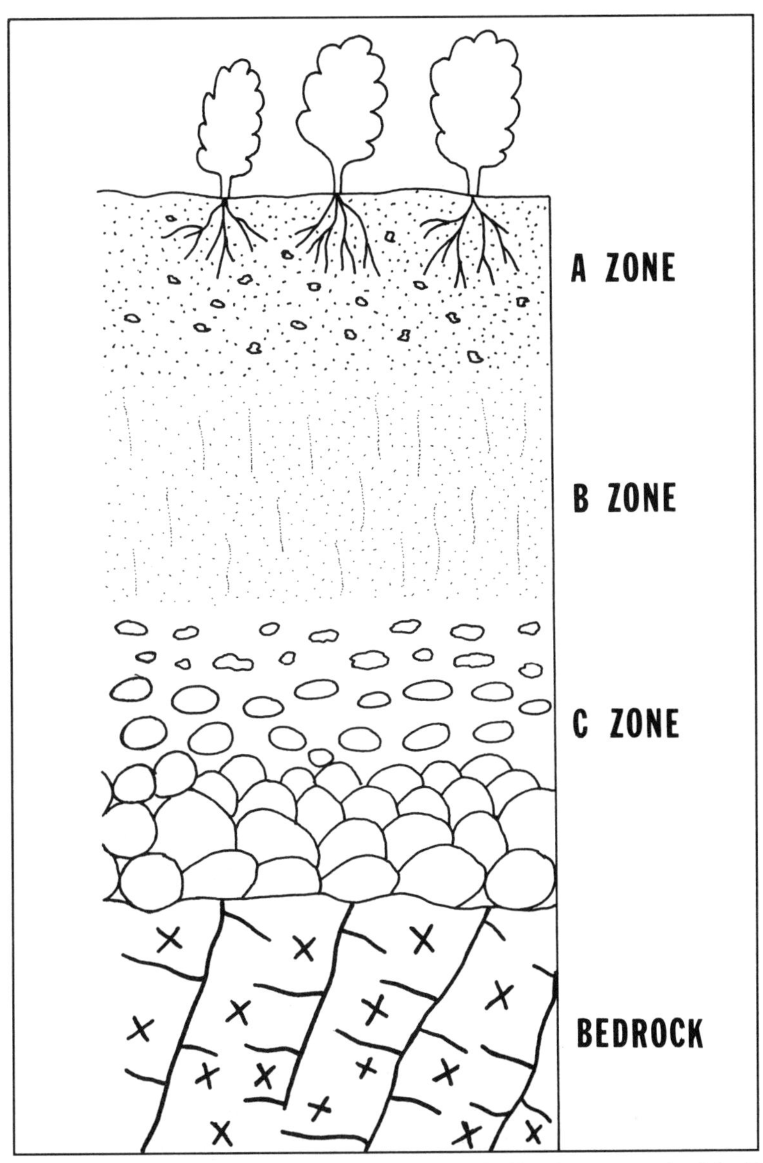

Figure 7–10 The soil profile. A zone—sand, silt, clay; organic rich. B zone—sand, silt, clay; organic poor. C zone—particles of parent rock plus material leached from above.

vegetative cover. Efforts to increase worldwide crop production by deforestation, irrigation, artificial fertilizers, genetic engineering, and other scientific methods (Fig. 7-11) might ultimately fail if in the long run the topsoil erodes away. A nearly 2 percent annual increase in food production

Figure 7–11 Soil testing at the Forestry Sciences Laboratory, Charleston, South Carolina. Courtesy of U.S. Forest Service

is required to meet the global demand, and most of this increase would have to be made up by new technology, especially since a significant portion of the world's cropland has already been lost.

Many rivers are becoming heavily sedimented due to topsoil erosion, particularly those in Africa, which has the worst erosion problem in the world. In the United States, eroding cropland is costing nearly a billion dollars annually due to polluted and sedimented rivers and lakes. The sediments also severely limit the life expectancy of dams erected for water projects used for irrigation. The best way to control silt buildup is to adopt effective soil-conservation measures in the watershed so that less topsoil will be lost to erosion.

TABLE 7–1 SUMMARY OF SOIL TYPES

	Climate			
	Temperate (humid) > 160 in. rainfall	**Temperate (dry) < 160 in. rainfall**	**Tropical (heavy rainfall)**	**Arctic or Desert**
Vegetation	Forest	Grass and brush	Grass and trees	Almost none, no humus development
Typical area	Eastern U.S.	Western U.S.		
Soil type	Pedalfer	Pedocal	Laterite	
Topsoil	Sandy, light-colored; acid	Enriched in calcite; white color	Enriched in iron and aluminum, brick-red color	No real soil forms because no organic material; chemical weathering very low
Subsoil	Enriched in aluminum, iron, and clay; brown color	Enriched in calcite; white color	All other elements removed by leaching	
Remarks	Extreme development in conifer forest; abundant humus makes ground-water acid; soil light gray due to lack of iron	Caliche—name applied to accumulation of calcite	Apparently bacteria destroy humus, no acid available to remove iron	

To keep up with an ever-growing human population, which adds another 90 million mouths to feed every year (equal to the combined populations of Mexico and Central America), many of the world's farmers have abandoned sound soil conservation practices in favor of more intensified farming methods. These include less rotation of crops, greater reliance on row crops, more plantings between fallow periods, and extensive use of chemical fertilizers instead of natural organic fertilizers that help bind the soil. Throughout the world, most of the arable land is already under cultivation, and efforts to cultivate substandard soils are leading to poor productivity and ultimately to abandonment, which in turn causes severe soil erosion. Marginal lands, which are often hilly, dry, or contain only thin, fragile topsoils and therefore erode easily, are also forced into production.

Over the last 150 years, the average soil depth in the United States has been cut in half through intensive agriculture. During the Dust Bowl years

Figure 7–12 Farm machinery buried during the 1930s Dust Bowl days. Courtesy of National Center for Atmospheric Research

of the 1930s—the worst ecological disaster of the century—tremendous quantities of topsoil were air-lifted out of the American Great Plains and deposited elsewhere, often burying areas under thick layers of sediment (Fig. 7-12). Massive dust storms raced across the prairie, carrying over 150,000 tons of sediment per square mile. Since then, improved agricultural practices have reduced this hazard in the United States as well as in other parts of the world. Unfortunately, many countries are still at risk from soil erosion, seriously undermining populations' ability to feed themselves.

In the 1980s, cropland in the United States shrank by 7 percent. During the 1988 drought, for the first time since World War II, Americans consumed more food than they grew. Despite expected rises in temperatures, increased evaporation rates, and changes in rainfall patterns, the United States should still be able to feed itself. However, there may be a limit to the nation's ability to produce excess food for export without imposing restrictions on its own population.

OVERIRRIGATION

The Fertile Crescent, known as the cradle of civilization, located between the Tigris and Euphrates Rivers in present-day Syria and Iraq, was once the

breadbasket of the Middle East, feeding a population of 17 to 25 million people as well as exporting food to surrounding regions. Today, the region is mostly an infertile desert due to overirrigation and soil salinization by Sumerian farmers 6,000 years ago. Even though its population is only about half what it once was, the area must now import large quantities of food.

Because Africa is prone to drought, it depends heavily on water projects to irrigate the parched land. Egypt's Nile River Delta (Fig. 7-13), whose rich soils began to form only 8,000 years ago, is one of the most developed irrigated areas in the world. Since the completion of the Aswan High Dam in the mid-1970s, which created Lake Nasser, only a trickle of the former Nile River reaches the Mediterranean Sea. Instead, most of its waters are used to irrigate some 20,000 square miles of farmland, encompassing an

Figure 7–13 Egypt's Nile Delta supports about 50 million people in a 7,500 square mile area. Courtesy of NASA

area about the size of West Virginia. On the border between Zambia and Zimbabwe, the Zambezi River was dammed to create Lake Kariba, the largest artificial reservoir in the world. However, efforts to convert western Africa's Sahel into a rice-growing region with irrigation are leading to severe soil salinization in poorly drained fields.

All the major rivers in South and Southeast Asia, including the Yangtze, the Mekong, the Irrawaddy, the Brahmaputra, the Ganges, and the Indus, have also been extensively developed for irrigation. China has a larger volume of regulated stream flow used mostly for irrigation than any other country in the world. Some 100,000 dams and reservoirs give China a total storage capacity of about 100 cubic miles of water. Russia is diverting two of its largest rivers, the Ob and Yenisea, to the southwest across warmer, more arable land through a series of giant dams and canals.

Figure 7–14a Border strip irrigation of crops in Imperial Valley, California. Photo by Robert Brandstead, courtesy of USDA–Soil Conservation Service

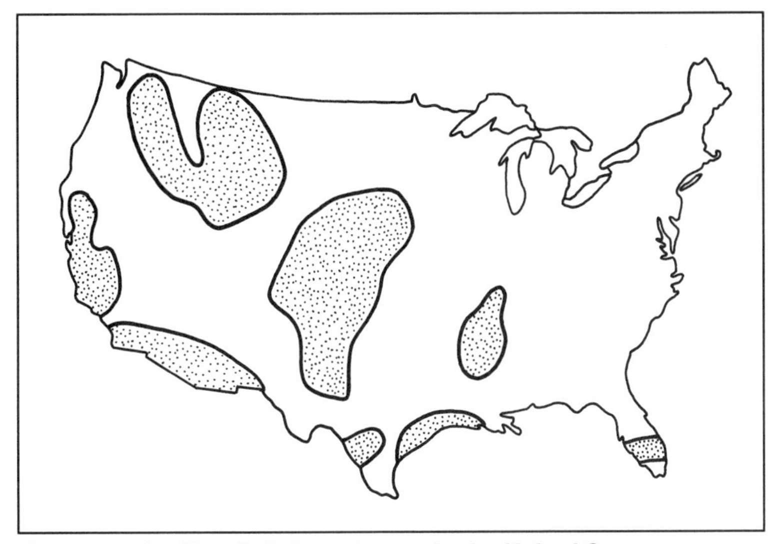

Figure 7–14b Heavily irrigated areas in the United States.

The world irrigates more than 10 percent of its cropland, requiring about 600 cubic miles of water annually. The United States irrigates nearly a quarter of its farmland (Figs. 7-14 a&b), tripling the amount of acreage irrigated since World War II. Irrigation has many advantages. Crops do not need to rely on undependable rainfall, more land can be brought under cultivation, and two or more crops can be grown in a single year. It also has many drawbacks, though. As mentioned, irrigation water has a high salt content, and if fields are not drained properly, salt buildup in the soil can ruin the land and crops can become stunted or die. Tens of thousands of acres of once-fertile land are destroyed by this process annually. By the end of the century, over half of all irrigated land could be rendered useless by salt accumulation in the soil.

Heavy use of irrigation, which not long ago turned vast stretches of the western desert of the United States into the world's most productive farmland, is ruining hundreds of thousands of acres. Irrigation is polluting marshes, rivers, lakes, and estuaries in California, Colorado, and other western states. Selenium, a naturally occurring chemical element in western topsoils, leached from soil on irrigated farms in the San Joaquin Valley of California has been implicated in causing deformities in nearby waterfowl, including twisted beaks, deformed wings, and missing eyes. The contaminated birds lay thin-shelled eggs that break easily, threatening whole generations of waterfowl.

The irrigation water gradually degrades the land by accumulating salts in the soil, such as sodium, calcium, and magnesium chlorides. By the turn of this century, at least one-third of California's farmland—some 1.5 million acres—could be destroyed by salt. Lower water availability in the spring and summer could also dramatically reduce crops. Meanwhile, the land in some regions contains selenium, arsenic, boron, and other naturally occurring poisons that are polluting the runoff.

With most good irrigated land already in production, farmers can ill afford to overcultivate, which results in oversalinization and, ultimately, abandonment. The problem is worse in arid regions because of the high natural salt content of the soil and the scarcity of rainfall, which is needed in good amounts to flush out the excess salts. Overirrigation on poorly drained fields also waterlogs the soil, causing root rot and stunted growth. Agricultural chemicals such as fertilizers, herbicides, and pesticides are carried off by the drainwater, polluting streams and rivers and finally the ocean, where high concentrations of chemicals are killing fish and other marine life, upon which much of the world depends for its survival. The worst example involves agricultural chemicals draining off the coasts of Sweden and Denmark, polluting the Kattegat Sea to such an extent that some 30 million sea creatures have died.

Groundwater irrigation is expensive, and usually only affluent nations can afford it on a large scale. The water is drawn from wells, in some cases thousands of feet deep, using large electric or diesel pumps, and is distributed over a circular area about half a mile across by a center pivot irrigation system. The overuse of groundwater leads to lowered water tables or total depletion of aquifers (Fig. 7-15). In many parts of the world, aquifers are

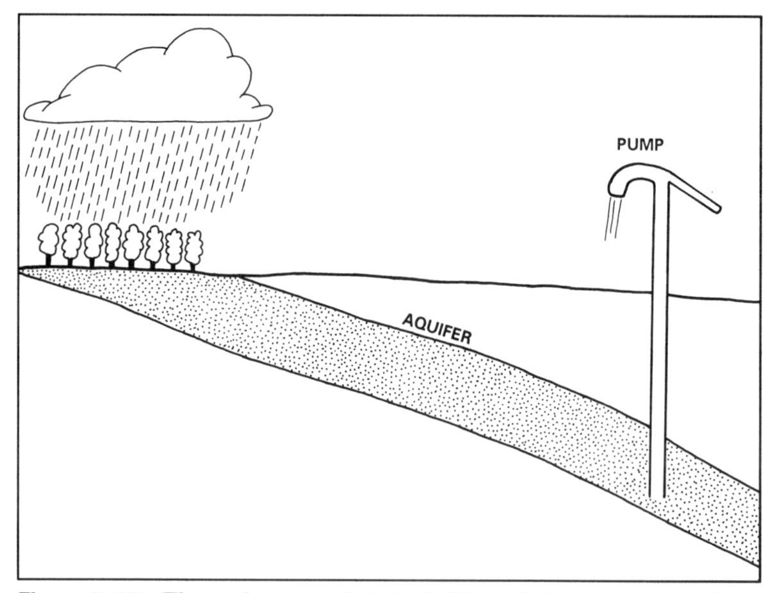

Figure 7–15 The recharge, or intake (left), and discharge, or outflow (right), of a groundwater acquifer.

being depleted faster than they are being replenished; eventually agriculture will become impossible in these regions.

Once an aquifer is depleted, subsidence causes sediment compaction and decreases the pore spaces between sediment grains where the water flows. The groundwater system can no longer carry its original capacity, causing wells to go dry. Throughout the world, groundwater aquifers are in danger of being depleted, which could spell disaster on a planet that continues to grow more densely populated.

PREVENTING FAMINE

The inhabitants of many African countries are malnourished. When the monsoon rains fail, people by the hundreds of thousands are put in danger

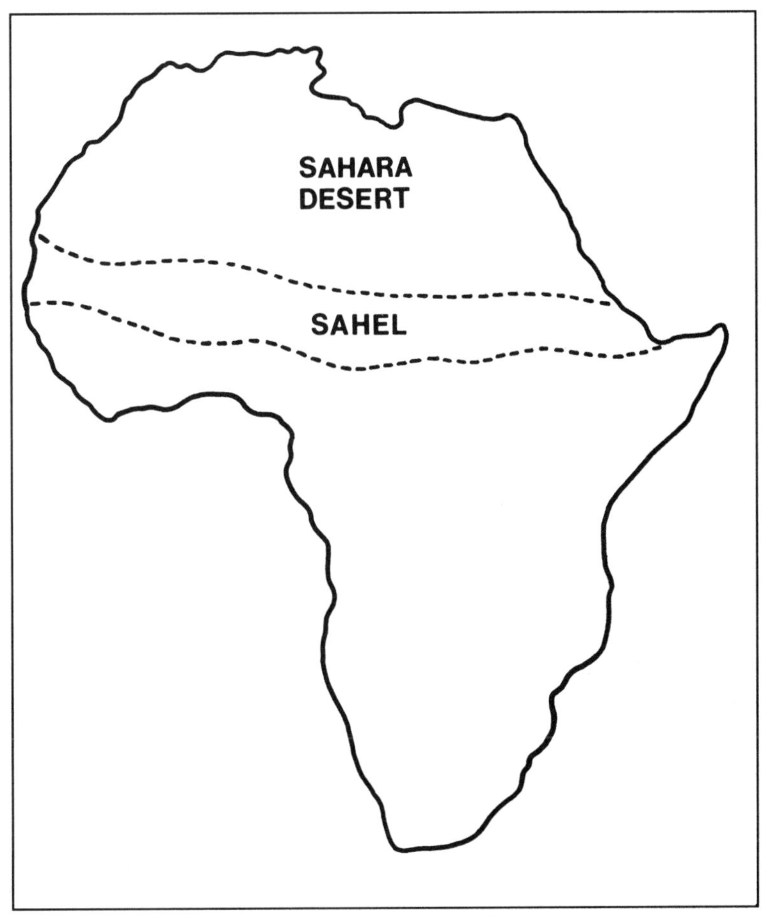

Figure 7–16 The Sahel region of Central Africa.

of dying of starvation. In 1984, the worst famine in African history killed about half a million people, mostly in Sudan and Ethiopia. Since the 1970s, central Africa lost much of its grazing land to the encroaching sands of the Sahara Desert. The southern boundaries of the Sahara crept 80 miles further south between 1980 and 1990. A vast belt of drought south of the Sahara, called the Sahel region (Fig. 7-16), is spreading gradually across the continent, parching the land and starving its inhabitants.

Droughts are a common occurrence in Africa. But the effects are steadily worsening because of Africa's deepening poverty, increasing population, and continuing land abuses. Changes in land use are altering the hydrologic cycle, causing a permanent decrease in rainfall and soil moisture. Much of the damage results from resource mismanagement, corruption, and civil war, which only aggravate the natural disasters that have always plagued the region. During the last drought, not only did people die in tragically large numbers but hundreds of thousands of livestock perished, further reducing the food store for the future.

Africa's dependence on foreign relief efforts continues to grow as the population expands, and natural disasters that have always beset the region are killing more and more people every year. Yet there is no definite evidence that the climatological mechanisms associated with droughts, floods, and tropical storms are changing. Africa is the world's poorest region and is the only area where the population, which is experiencing the fastest growth rate of any continent in human history, is rapidly outpacing the food supply. If populations keep growing, by late in the next century, Africans, which now comprise about 10 percent of the population, could constitute one-quarter of the human race.

8

HABITAT DESTRUCTION

We have inherited a world with a wide variety of environments—perhaps a wider variety than at any other time in geologic history. These habitats in turn support large numbers of diverse plant and animal species. At the same time humans first appeared, some 2 million years ago, over 70 percent of today's species came into existence. Currently, however, important ecosystems like the tropical rain forests are rapidly disappearing due to people's destructive activities. Humans are encroaching upon the habitats of other species in a desperate race to support themselves by primitive slash-and-burn agriculture, resulting in the loss of valuable forests and the species they support (Fig. 8-1). If the clearing of world's woodlands continues at its present furious pace, only a few isolated stands of trees will remain and more than half of all species will be gone.

WORLD ENVIRONMENTS

The Earth's land surface is made up of roughly one-third desert; one-third forests, savanna, and wetlands; and one-fifth glacial ice and tundra (Fig. 8-2), with the rest occupied by humans. About 10 percent of the land surface is commandeered for farmland and about 25 percent for pasture. Some 400

Figure 8–1 Deforestation in the tropics. Courtesy of National Center for Atmospheric Research

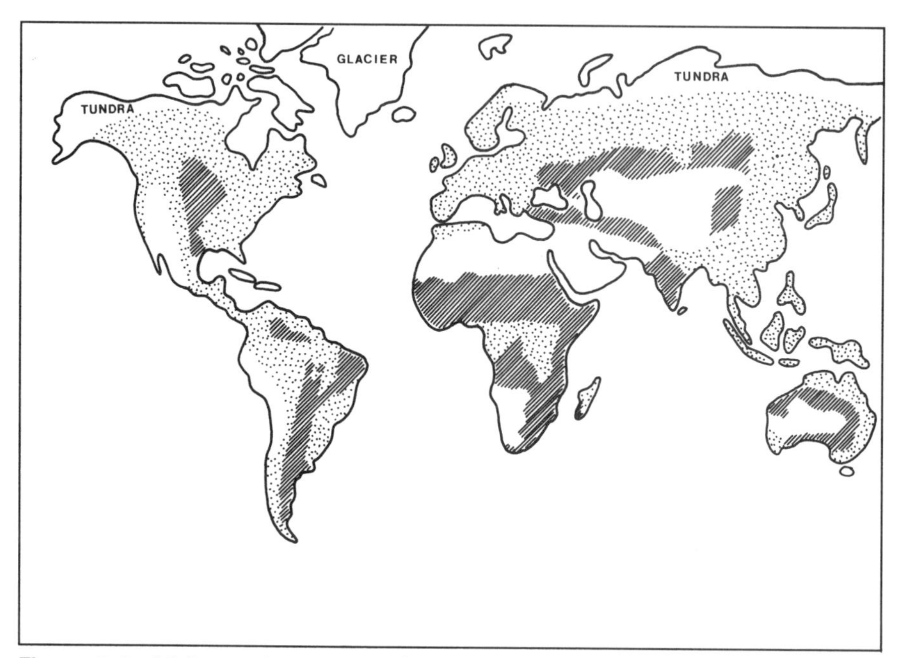

Figure 8–2 Major environments of the world. White areas represent deserts, hash marked areas represent savannas, and stippled areas represent forests.

square miles (20 miles by 20 miles) of arable land are required to feed 1 million people. With a doubling of the human population, either more land must be cultivated or twice as much food must be grown per acre. In the former case, more forests would have to be cleared and more wetlands drained. In the latter case, such intensive agriculture would ultimately destroy the land.

Globally, an area nearly twice the size of the United States has become desertified, mostly through the abuse of land. At the current rate, in the next two decades perhaps as much as 500,000 square miles (an area about the size of Alaska) of agricultural land could be rendered useless. As populations continue to grow and lay waste to the landscape, man-made deserts will continue to spread over much of the Earth's surface.

Tropical rain forests cover only about 7 percent of the land surface (Fig. 8-3), yet they contain two-thirds or more of all species. Plants and animals of the rain forests are being crowded out by the encroachment of humans into their habitats, resulting in the destruction of ecological niches and the pollution of the environment with industrial and agricultural poisons. Already, half the rain forests of the world have been destroyed for agriculture and timber harvest.

About a third of the world's land surface is wilderness, with little signs of human presence. Except for a few scattered outposts, the ice continent of Antarctica (Fig. 8-4) is practically all wilderness—a situation that could well change as nations begin to explore for oil and minerals. Several broad belts of wilderness wind their way around the globe. One stretches across upper North America and the northernmost reaches of Eurasia. Another runs southwest from far eastern Asia through Tibet, Afghanistan, and Saudi Arabia into Africa. The forbidding Sahara Desert in northern Africa and the

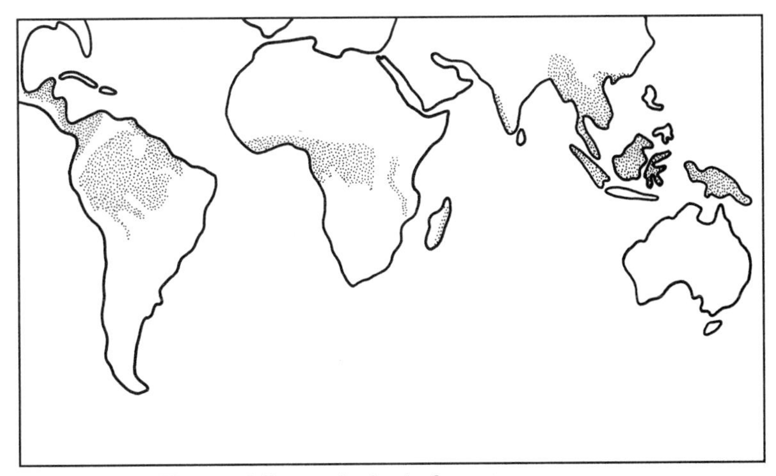

Figure 8–3 The world's tropical rain forests.

Figure 8–4 A Coast Guard icebreaker clears a channel into McMurdo Sound, Antarctica. Photo by M. Mullen, courtesy of U.S. Navy

great central desert of Australia are additional wilderness areas. Wild patches also exist in other parts of Africa, around the Amazon, and along the Andes Mountains of South America.

DEFORESTATION

Our planet is in danger of losing the battle for its forests and wildlife. Only about 3.8 million square miles of tropical rain forest—an area about the size of the United States—remain in the entire world. Tropical rain forests like those in the Amazon Basin of South America (Fig. 8-5) are decreasing at the alarming rate of about 75 acres per minute, or about 40 million acres annually—an area about the size of the state of Georgia. At the present rate of deforestation, most of the world's rain forests could completely disappear by the middle of the next century.

Currently the world's tropical forests have been reduced by about half. The tropical rain forest along the Atlantic coast of Brazil has dwindled to less than 1 percent of its original cover. In its place is a huge man-made desert. The montane forests along the flanks of the Andes Mountains are also severely threatened, with those in the north already 90 percent deforested. Unlike the Amazon rain forests, the montane forests are extremely delicate, and pressures from a burgeoning population threaten what little is left.

Figure 8–5 The Amazon rain forest of South America.

Over 80 percent of Mexico's tropical rain forest has been destroyed. The forest cover of the Ivory Coast in western Africa has decreased by 75 percent since 1960. In terms of percentage of deforestation, continental Southeast Asia is losing a larger proportion of its forests each year. Indonesia has lost most of its rain forests, up to 2,500 square miles a year, due to resettlement from the overcrowded main island of Java.

The rain forests are being cleared mostly for agricultural purposes. About 15 percent of the trees are cut down for timber production, much of which is wasted by inefficient harvesting and milling methods. Logging is often

the first step toward deforestation, as loggers build roads into the forest to pave the way for farmers. Forest clear-cutting is a tragic waste of a natural resource, and impoverished countries lose an important source of revenue as trees go up in smoke. Many countries richly endowed with forests, including Central and South America, Southeast Asia, and Africa, have created economic incentives to stimulate rapid depletion of their timber resources and the conversion of forest land to agriculture and other uses.

Throughout the world, billions of dollars worth of timber is often simply burned. In the Amazon jungle of Brazil, some 20 million acres of forests go up in smoke each year. Because of a poor economy, many Brazilians are being forced to leave the cities and settle in the frontier regions to eke out a living. The tropical rain forests are being cleared on an unprecedented scale, mostly for pasture to graze cattle, whose meat is sold to more affluent nations. Despite pleas from biologists, a large part of Hawaii's last remain-

Figure 8–6 Viewed from the space shuttle *Discovery* in December 1988, the Amazon basin of South America is obscured by smoke from clearing and burning of the tropical rain forest. Courtesy of NASA

ing lowland rain forest has been harvested to supply fuel for electrical power generation, a tragic waste of a valuable resource.

Deforestation results in large part from the consequences of poor forest management by governments with significant economic problems. Less than 1 percent of the remaining tropical forests is being actively managed for sustained productivity. Deforestation has a severe environmental impact on soil, water quality, and local climate. Fishes in rivers and lakes are damaged by increased sedimentation from soil erosion in deforested areas. Some tropical forest fires are so enormous they create massive smoke clouds (Fig. 8-6). The smoke in the Amazon jungle is often so thick and extensive it has closed commercial airports in northern Brazil due to poor visibility.

Many forests in the Northern Hemisphere are succumbing to air pollution and acid rain (Fig. 8-7). The Swiss Alps are threatened with deforestation from air pollution generated largely by heavy automobile traffic. Ironically, the tourist trade the mountains help foster is in the process of destroying their great beauty. More than half of all alpine trees are sick, and 15 percent are dead or dying. The weakened state of these forests leaves them susceptible to disease. This might explain why over 50 percent of the native plants and animals considered endangered or threatened are alpine species.

The United States retains only about 15 percent of its once vast sea of forests. The remaining forests are rapidly being depleted for timber prod-

Figure 8–7 Small open-top chambers for acid rain study. Photo by Dorothy Andrake, courtesy of U.S. Forest Service

Figure 8–8 The Amazon River basin shown on a cloudy day during the rainy season. Courtesy of NASA

ucts. Some 60,000 acres of the old-growth forests, mainly in the Pacific Northwest, are cut annually for lumber that is mostly exported to countries along the Pacific rim, principally Japan, to support a building boom. The timber is usually shipped in its raw form rather than processed into lumber and other products that would improve the economy of the region.

The temperate forests of the higher latitudes are in danger of destruction as well. Over the past two decades, the growth rate and general health of forests in the northeastern United States, eastern Canada, and many parts of central Europe have been declining. Several factors are responsible for destroying the forests (along with water resources), the worst of which is acid rain. The acids are generated by large industrial centers and precipitated some distance away. The acidified runoff flows into streams and lakes and percolates into the soil, where it damages plant roots, kills nitrogen-fixing bacteria, and leaches out valuable soil nutrients. The direct contact of acids with foliage also destroys trees as well as agricultural crops.

The soil underlying the rain forests is generally of poor quality, and the fertilizing effect of the ash from burning trees is effective for no more than a few years due to the leaching of nutrients by heavy rains. After intensive

agriculture robs the soil of its nutrients, farmers, especially in Amazonia, often abandon their fields and clear the forests for more land. When the rains return, flash floods wash away the denuded soil down to bedrock, and the rain forest has no chance of recovery. About half the precipitation in the rain forest originates from the forest itself due to the high transpiration rates of the dense vegetation (Fig. 8-8). The destruction of large parts of the rain forests changes precipitation patterns, with the potential of turning wide areas into man-made deserts that affect the entire global climate system.

The rapid decline of the rain forests is mostly a consequence of modern methods of timber harvesting, including the widespread use of chainsaws and bulldozers. Lumber companies employ timber harvesting equipment that snips trees off at the base with giant shears. Wood chippers grind a 100-foot tree into pulp in half a minute. After the most desirable trees are removed, unwanted trees and brush are set ablaze.

The bare ground, denuded of all vegetation, is left unattended, making the land vulnerable to flash floods and severe soil erosion (Fig. 8-9). Soil erosion caused by large-scale deforestation can overload rivers with sediment, causing considerable problems downstream. Monsoon floodwaters cascading down the denuded foothills of the Himalayas of northern India and carried to the Bay of Bengal by the Ganges and Brahmaputra rivers have devastated Bangladesh, where several thousand people lost their lives to floods in August 1989. South America's Amazon River is now forced to carry more water during the flood season due to deforestation at its headwaters.

Figure 8–9 Deep sheet erosion in which 2 to 3 feet of soil have been removed from a steep embankment, Carter County, Tennessee. Photo by A. Keith, courtesy of USGS

WILDLIFE HABITATS

The Earth is losing valuable plant and animal life at a rate of 100 or more species daily, due to the destruction of wildlife habitats. Already half the bird species of Polynesia have been eliminated by overhunting and destruction of native forests. Throughout the world, the die-off of species is thousands of times greater than the natural rate of extinction prior to the appearance of humans. Biologists are in a desperate race to classify as many species as possible before more disappear. Amazingly, over 90 percent of all species have not yet been described.

Three-quarters of the global deforestation is conducted by landless, poverty-stricken people in a desperate race for survival. As much as 70

Figure 8–10 An artist's rendition of Landsat-D satellite used to map global deforestation. Courtesy of NASA

percent of the wood harvested in poor tropical countries is used locally for firewood. Because of the scarcity of firewood, the only source of fuel for heating and cooking in impoverished regions, the forests of Africa are rapidly being depleted. As the forests recede, severe firewood shortages loom ahead.

Africa, once a sea of wild animals surrounding a few islands of humanity, now has only a few enclaves of animals surrounded by a mass of people. The African birthrate, the highest in the world, could triple the population of the continent to 1.6 billion people by the year 2025. Such a large population could potentially multiply the present rate of destruction, leaving little hope for African wildlife.

Tropical rain forests in the New World once covered 3 million square miles. That area has now dwindled to about a third of its original cover. In addition, as much as three-quarters of the tropical rain forests of Africa have been destroyed. The detection, identification, and measurement of the symptoms of forest decline using satellite technology is urgently needed (Fig. 8-10). Such observations can provide the means to assess and monitor forest destruction on a global scale, giving governments critical information to help them reduce forest destruction.

Rain forests are the homes of about 80,000 plant species. Certain exotic plants are rapidly disappearing, and 7 percent of all plant species are likely to become extinct by the end of this century if current trends continue. Some plants have an important medicinal value. Half of all pharmaceuticals are manufactured from natural herbs, most of which live only in the tropical rain forests. Therefore, with the destruction of the tropical rain forests, humanity loses the ability to find new cures for fatal diseases.

In the United States alone, up to 10 percent of plant species are destined for extinction by the end of this century. The native plants risk extinction from habitat loss by the destruction of forests, the extension of agriculture, and the spread of urbanization. About 3 percent of the nation's land area is covered by buildings and roads. Growing cities sacrifice many trees to development, and their loss contributes to the "heat island effect," making pavement and buildings heat reservoirs. The heat gain requires additional artificial air conditioning to replace the natural cooling effects of the vegetation, placing higher demands on energy resources.

If global warming trends continue, by the middle of the next century the forests of the southern states could disappear, to be replaced by grasslands. The great forests of eastern North America could shift northward as much as 600 miles. Pine forests could take over stands of spruce in New England and the Appalachian Mountains. Pines could reach as far north as the arctic tundra. The prairies of the Midwest could sweep eastward as far as Pennsylvania and New York.

As the climate warms and the forests dry out, extensive forest fires could lay waste huge tracts of valuable forested land, as they did at Yellowstone

Figure 8–11 Forest fires in Yellowstone National Park destroyed nearly half the forested land in the summer and fall of 1988. Courtesy of National Park Service

National Park during the summer and fall of 1988 (Fig. 8-11). If global temperatures rise too rapidly, forests might fail to keep up with the movement of climate zones toward higher latitudes, causing a further decline of the world's forested regions along with the species they support. The resulting ecological change could take 500 years or more to stabilize, and conditions could rival those at the end of the last ice age 10,000 years ago.

CLIMATE EFFECTS

The forests of the world have a major effect on the global climate. The loss of forests increases the Earth's surface albedo, allowing more sunlight to be reflected into space. Thus, deforestation could cause global cooling that might counteract greenhouse warming caused by pollution. The loss of solar energy from deforestation could change precipitation patterns, causing decreased rainfall, especially in the rain forests themselves. These drought conditions could further stress the trees, making them more susceptible to disease.

Soot from forest fires and brushfires (Fig. 8-12) absorbs sunlight, heating the atmosphere and producing a temperature imbalance, which causes temperatures to rise with altitude—just the opposite of what should hap-

Figure 8–12 A forest fire in Washoe County, Nevada that destroyed approximately 1,500 acres. Courtesy of USDA–Soil Conservation Service

pen. Large quantities of atmospheric soot generated by massive forest fires could thus result in abnormal weather throughout the world.

The harvesting of forests, the extension of agriculture, and the destruction of wetlands speed the decay of dead organic matter in the soil, releasing massive amounts of carbon dioxide into the atmosphere. The destruction of forests alone is responsible for injecting some 2.5 billion tons of carbon into the atmosphere. Moreover, agricultural lands, which also produce carbon dioxide during cultivation, do not store nearly as much carbon as the forests they replace. Forests conduct more photosynthesis for a given area than any other form of vegetation. They incorporate from 10 to 20 times more carbon per acre than cropland or pasture and contain as much carbon as the entire atmosphere. The clearing of land for agriculture, especially in the tropics, is the largest source of carbon released into the atmosphere by living organisms and soils.

Deforestation accounts for up to a third of the total amount of carbon dioxide and up to half the methane released into the atmosphere. As the carbon stored in the trees escapes into the air, the concurrent reduction of the forests is weakening their ability to remove excess atmospheric carbon dioxide, with the potential for causing global warming. Although the forests

of North America and Europe have a net accumulation of carbon, the absorption of excess carbon dioxide is insignificant compared to the losses in tropical regions. Recently, however, the uptake of carbon dioxide has ceased because of massive increases in tree dieback and logging in the northern boreal forests of North America and Eurasia.

Another threat posed by deforestation is the release of nitrous oxide into the atmosphere, possibly damaging the stratospheric ozone layer, which filters out harmful solar ultraviolet radiation (Fig. 8-13). Forest clear-cutting encourages soil bacteria to produce nitrous oxide that escapes into the air. The tremendous heat generated by burning forests combines nitrogen and oxygen to form nitrous oxide, and a significant amount of this gas enters the upper atmosphere, where it destroys ozone.

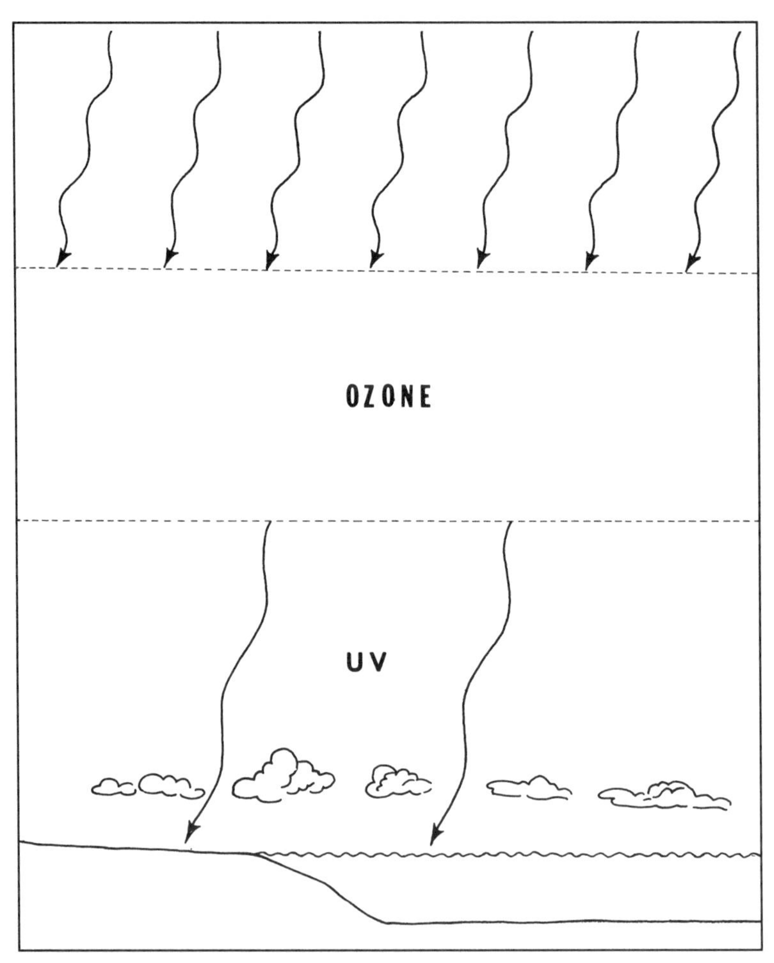

Figure 8–13 The ozone layer filters out harmful solar ultraviolet radiation.

The number of termites is rapidly rising because of deforestation. About three-quarters of a ton of termites exists for every person on Earth. But as deforestation escalates, the population of termites could increase many times over. Termites ingest as much as two-thirds of all terrestrial carbon, about 1 percent of which is converted into methane, another potent greenhouse gas.

Methane production is increasing at a rate of about 1 percent per year, or about twice as fast as carbon dioxide. Methane is also about 20 times more efficient as a greenhouse gas. In future years, methane and other trace greenhouse gases might together contribute more to global warming than carbon dioxide. In addition, large numbers of cattle raised on cleared forested land contribute substantial amounts of atmospheric methane during their digestive process. With one bovine for every four people, they could play a significant role in changing the world's climate.

REFORESTATION

While alternative nonpolluting energy sources are being developed, we could curtail carbon dioxide buildup in the atmosphere by planting trees. By doubling the volume of forest growth each year, the major fossil-fuel-consuming nations could delay the onset of a possible global warming by perhaps a decade or more. However, the destruction of the tropical rain forests would have to be halted as well. A forest covering nearly 3 million square miles, an area roughly the size of the United States, would be required to fully restore the Earth's carbon dioxide balance. This equals the extent of all tropical forests cleared since the dawn of agriculture.

By planting additional trees, we could add enough forest growth to absorb the excess carbon dioxide being discharged into the atmosphere by human activities. Replanting perhaps as many as 100 million trees would remove about 18 million tons of carbon dioxide from the atmosphere each year. In the United States, lumber companies reseed the clear-cut areas to ensure a future supply of timber products. Unfortunately, this practice leads to closely spaced stands of single species of pine in places that once supported a large assortment of tree species—trees that provided a variety of habitats for other species of plants and animals. Some areas in the Pacific Northwest that were clear-cut 30 years ago are still barren because of severe soil erosion. In the Appalachian Mountains (Fig. 8-14), forests clear-cut nearly a century ago and allowed to grow back naturally have yet to return to their former condition.

Cutting old-growth forests adds carbon dioxide to the atmosphere, by combustion, decomposition, and processing of wood products, which contributes to the greenhouse effect. A replanted forest requires about 200 years for its storage capacity to approach that of an old-growth forest, where

Figure 8–14 The foothills of Blue Ridge and Piedmont Plateau, Buncombe County, North Carolina.
Courtesy of USGS

trees are among the oldest living things on Earth, often surviving for thousands of years.

Fast-growing loblolly pines need 25 to 30 years to mature. But in the past two decades, loblolly growth rates in the American South have declined by as much as 15 percent as a result of air pollution, mostly surface ozone (a major air pollutant not to be confused with stratospheric ozone). In addition, ozone is responsible for about 90 percent of crop failures resulting from air pollution in the United States. High ozone levels also reduce photosynthesis and increase cell damage in sequoia seedlings, dramatically reducing their survival rate. Giant sequoias were quite common in the past, but today their range is confined to a 30-mile-wide noncontinuous strip, running some 500 miles along the Pacific Coast from northern California to south of Big Sur.

New trees require two to three decades to mature, and it is uncertain whether the human race has that much time to solve the carbon dioxide problem. Furthermore, immature trees do not absorb as much carbon dioxide as those they replace. For much of the world, deforestation has destroyed the topsoil, so replanting trees is no longer an option. However, new forests could be planted on numerous degraded lands that are no longer agriculturally productive (Fig. 8-15).

Aware of the bleak future that awaits many species, several nations have set aside game preserves in an attempt to halt the tide of habitat destruction

Figure 8–15 Ruins of an old cabin and deep eroded gullies on bared slopes below spruce woods in Carter County, Tennessee. Photo by A. Keith, courtesy of USGS

and extinction. Yet even these areas represent less than 1 percent of the remaining forests. The amount of forested land in the United States and a few other countries has actually increased in recent years. The United States Forest Service has taken millions of acres of forest land out of multiple use and established wilderness areas. Unfortunately, the forests surrounding these enclaves are still in danger of being destroyed.

9

BIOLOGICAL EXTINCTION

The overpopulation of the Earth by a single species, representing only one out of several million species, is forcing the rest of the living world to move aside. Humans are rather large animals and command a major share of the Earth's natural resources. No other sizable mammal even approaches the number of human beings alive today. Conversely, the populations of many animals have fallen so low they can no longer maintain their numbers and are in danger of extinction.

Many endangered species exist only in captivity, where their future depends on captive breeding programs. However, breeding wild animals in captivity produces changes that sometimes interfere with successful habitation when these animals are reintroduced into the wild. Clearly, the time to save a species is when it is common. Once a species' numbers dwindle, preventing its extinction can be very expensive and is often a losing battle.

PREHISTORIC EXTINCTIONS

The most recent mass extinction occurred at the end of the last ice age about 11,000 years ago. This was an unusual extinction event because it affected

Figure 9–1 Large mammals that went extinct in North America following the last ice age.

only large terrestrial plant-eating mammals called megaherbivores. The majority of mammals affected were large plant-eaters weighing over 100 pounds—many weighing as much as a ton or more. Eurasia lost its woolly rhinos, mammoths, and Irish elk. Simultaneously, Africa lost its great buffalo, giant hartebeests, and giant horses. North America lost its giant ground sloths, woolly mammoths, and mastodons (Fig. 9-1). The die-out of these animals also led to the extinction of their main predators, the dire wolf and the saber-toothed tiger.

The extinctions might have been caused by a dramatic shift in climate. When the glaciers retreated at the end of the last ice age, the global environment readjusted to the changing climate. Mixed habitats became more uniform, with shrunken forests and expanded grasslands (Fig. 9-2). These changing climatic conditions disrupted the food chains of many large animals and, deprived of their food sources, the megaherbivores simply vanished.

Humans contributed to the extinctions. By this time, they had become proficient hunters and roamed northward following the retreating glaciers.

Figure 9–2 Grass-covered glaciated topography, Glacier County, Montana. Photo by H. E. Malde, courtesy of USGS

On their journey, they encountered an abundance of wildlife, many species of which they totally decimated. Some 35 classes of mammals and 10 classes of birds became extinct almost simultaneously in North America. These extinctions took place between 12,000 and 10,000 years ago, with the greatest die-out peaking around 11,000 years ago. However, unlike earlier episodes of mass extinctions, such as the disappearance of the dinosaurs (Fig. 9-3), this event did not significantly affect small mammals, amphibians, reptiles, and marine invertebrates.

From 11,500 to 11,000 years ago, many parts of North America were occupied by ice age peoples, whose presence is attested to by spear points found among the remains of giant mammals, including mammoths, mastodons, tapirs, native horses, and camels. These people originated in Asia, crossed into North America over a land bridge formed by the draining of the Bering Sea during the last ice age, and moved through an ice-free corridor east of the Canadian Rockies. When they entered North America, they found a land populated with as many as 100 million large mammals similar to those decimated in Europe and Asia.

The climate change resulting from the transition from ice age conditions to the present warm interglacial period caused sea levels to rise and water levels in rivers in lakes to fall over much of North America after the glaciers melted. Large mammals congregating at the few remaining water holes might have been vulnerable to human hunting pressures. With plentiful prey and little exposure to new diseases, human populations soared, and people spread southward, leaving many big-game extinctions behind them.

Historically, humans have accounted for the extinction of many island species. Species living on islands are particularly vulnerable to human predation because they have nowhere to flee. Before the end of the last ice age, humans were living on the island of Cyprus in the eastern Mediterranean. The landing of people on the island coincided with the disappearance of the pygmy hippopotamus, which was about the size of a small pig and once roamed freely on Cyprus and other nearby islands. One site contained a large number of pygmy hippo skull bones, along with rock flakes supposedly made by human hunters. Apparently, this was a refuse pile, indicating that people had a hand in the extinction of the Cyprus hippos.

Animals occupying islands often develop unique characteristics that differentiate them from their mainland relatives. For example, island birds are frequently flightless because they no longer need to take to the air to escape from predators. Often, species became extinct because of the de-

Figure 9–3 All species of dinosaurs went extinct within a relatively short period, due to a number of suspected causes, both terrestrial and extraterrestrial.

struction of their habitats or the introduction of predators or competing species, as was the situation in Australia, where rabbits overran the continent. In many cases, the animals were senselessly slaughtered for no apparent reason except possibly for their fur or plumage.

Extinctions were also massive in Australia, possibly perpetrated by the ancestors of the Aborigines. The isolated continent of Australia is inhabited by many strange animals; it seems to be a throwback to a time 40 million years ago when large, bizarre mammals roamed the Earth. Australia was separated from the rest of the world until the early arrival of humans about 60,000 years ago. When people migrated to Australia, the continent lost its giant marsupials, including the giant kangaroos. Australia also lost over 80 percent of its large mammals and a significant number of bird species.

PRESENT-DAY EXTINCTIONS

Humans are the most adaptable of all species, capable of living in the most diverse environments. We are also the only creatures on Earth to have brought about the extinctions of large numbers of other animal species (Fig. 9-4). For the first time in geologic history, plants are also being extinguished in large numbers. Those plants and animals that are not directly beneficial to humans are forced aside as growing populations continue to squander

Figure 9-4 Florida manatees are threatened with extinction by reckless motorboaters.

Figure 9–5 Sharks have survived extinctions over the past 400 million years.

the Earth's space and resources and contaminate the environment with industrial and agricultural pollution.

Wherever humans have gone, they have wiped out entire species of mammals, birds, reptiles, and fish, along with indigenous groups of their fellow humans. From 1600 to 1900, during a period of extensive maritime exploration, humans eliminated 75 known species, mostly birds and mammals. The passenger pigeons that once darkened the skies over North America by the billions during colonial times had completely died out by 1914 due to overhunting and destruction of natural habitats. We continue to destroy life on every continent and island we inhabit, but now we do it on a much larger scale simply because there are so many more of us.

Freshwater fish species are rapidly disappearing worldwide from deforestation, which increases sedimentation, and from acid rain, which disrupts the pH balance of lakes and streams. Nor are the oceans immune to human pressures, and previously large fisheries, the source of half of human's dietary protein, have been seriously depleted to feed ever-growing human populations. Even the great sharks (Fig. 9-5), which have been successful predators for the last 400 million years, are succumbing to overfishing.

Birds too are at great risk, and humans have forced more than 100 bird species into extinction over the past 400 years. Half the Hawaiian bird population collapsed following Polynesian habitation about 1,600 years ago. In more recent times, bird populations have further declined by about 15 percent. These extinctions are typical of the impact of human settlement in island communities.

Figure 9–6 Antarctic penguins often succumb to toxins from distant sources.

Some 2,000 species of birds that existed a few thousand years ago—about a fifth of all birds—have fallen victim to prehistoric exterminations. An additional 20 percent of bird species are presently endangered or are at imminent risk of extinction due to human activities that have directly or indirectly altered the environment in ways detrimental to birds. Large, flightless birds, like the now-extinct dodo and the great auk, are especially vulnerable. Antarctic penguins (Fig. 9-6), which were thought to be relatively safe from human encroachment into their environment, have been found with high levels of DDT from distant sources in their livers.

The reasons for the extinctions are numerous. Birds, along with other valuable species, are going extinct due to overhunting, the introduction of species that prey on or directly compete with indigenous species, the destruction of habitats by deforestation and wetland drainage, and the collapse of food chains, which disrupts predator-prey relationships. All species depend on other species for their survival. Due to the interrelatedness of species, if too many in a certain habitat become extinct, the remaining animals are at risk of extinction through a "domino effect." If this process continues globally due to human disruption, the damage could initiate the collapse of biology and incur the worst extinction event in the history of the planet.

The interrelationships among species, and between species and their environments, are highly complex and difficult to understand. However, it is becoming more and more apparent that the destruction of large numbers of the world's species would not only lower species diversity but would allow animals commonly considered pests to flourish, because their natural predator would be eliminated. Therefore, the destruction of large numbers of species would leave us with a world entirely different from the one we presently occupy. Indeed, it is doubtful that human beings could survive in such a world, because biological support systems such as critical food chains would be severely damaged.

The current extinction rate is thousands of times greater than the rate of extinction that prevailed prior to the appearance of human beings. Present-day extinctions, in which thousands of species are vanishing yearly, are forced extinctions that result from destructive human activities. If the spiral of human population growth and environmental destruction continues out of control, possibly by the middle of the next century half of all species living today will be extinct.

Already, many species nearing extinction can be found only in captivity, and these represent only a small fraction of all endangered species. Once the population of a species drops below a certain critical level, the likelihood of extinction increases due to a greatly reduced gene pool. Inbreeding exposes species to genetic defects that decimate populations. Also, once a species loses its genetic variability it is doomed because it can no longer adapt to changes in its environment.

CAUSES OF EXTINCTION

When human populations were small and the environmental impacts of human activities were negligible, other species were virtually unaffected by them. However, the introduction of agriculture spurred a fundamental change in human behavior, as people learned ways to profit from and conquer nature. The Industrial Revolution sparked another major change in human culture and had profound global consequences. These developments resulted in phenomenal population growth, and the pressure of the human presence was felt by the rest of the living world.

The extinctions of the past (Fig. 9-7) were caused by natural phenomena, including changing climatic and environmental conditions. Present-day

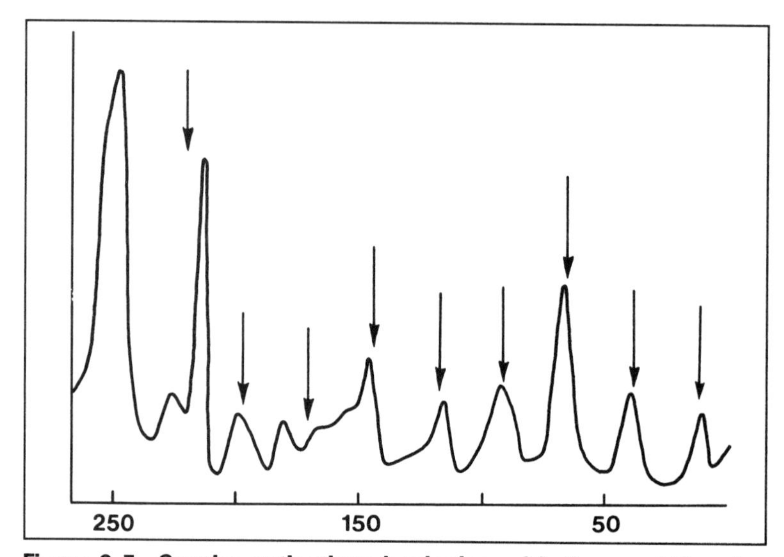

Figure 9–7 Species extinctions beginning with the great Permian die-out 250 million years ago.

extinctions are caused by destructive human activities, which some people have attempted to justify by implying that humans are also part of the natural world and thus have the right to use the Earth's resources as they please. Unfortunately, this attitude has been very destructive to the Earth and its plant and animal life.

TABLE 9–1 EVOLUTION AND EXTINCTION OF MAJOR ORGANISMS

Organism	Evolution	Extinction
Marine invertebrates	Lower Paleozoic	Permian
Foraminiferans	Silurian	Permian & Triassic
Graptolites	Ordovician	Silurian & Devonian
Brachiopods	Ordovician	Devonian & Carboniferous
Nautiloids	Ordovician	Mississippian
Ammonoids	Devonian	Upper Cretaceous
Trilobites	Cambrian	Carboniferous & Permian
Crinoids	Ordovician	Upper Permian

Organism	Evolution	Extinction
Fishes	Devonian	Pennsylvanian
Land plants	Devonian	Permian
Insects	Upper Paleozoic	
Amphibians	Pennsylvania	Permian–Triassic
Reptiles	Permian	Upper Cretaceous
Mammals	Paleocene	Pleistocene

A possible prelude to global extinction is the alarming disappearance throughout the world of frogs and other amphibians that have existed for more than 300 million years. Moreover, amphibians are disappearing from nature preserves, where little human perturbation occurs. These creatures could be sounding an early warning that the planet is in grave danger from acid rain and stratospheric ozone depletion.

BIOLOGICAL COMMUNITIES

Wetlands are among the richest plant and animal communities in the world (Fig. 9-8), supporting large numbers of diverse species. Many wetlands in the United States, like the great Florida Everglades (Fig. 9-9), have been

Figure 9–8 An estuary of Twelvemile Creek, Niagara County, New York. Photo by G. K. Gilbert, courtesy of USGS

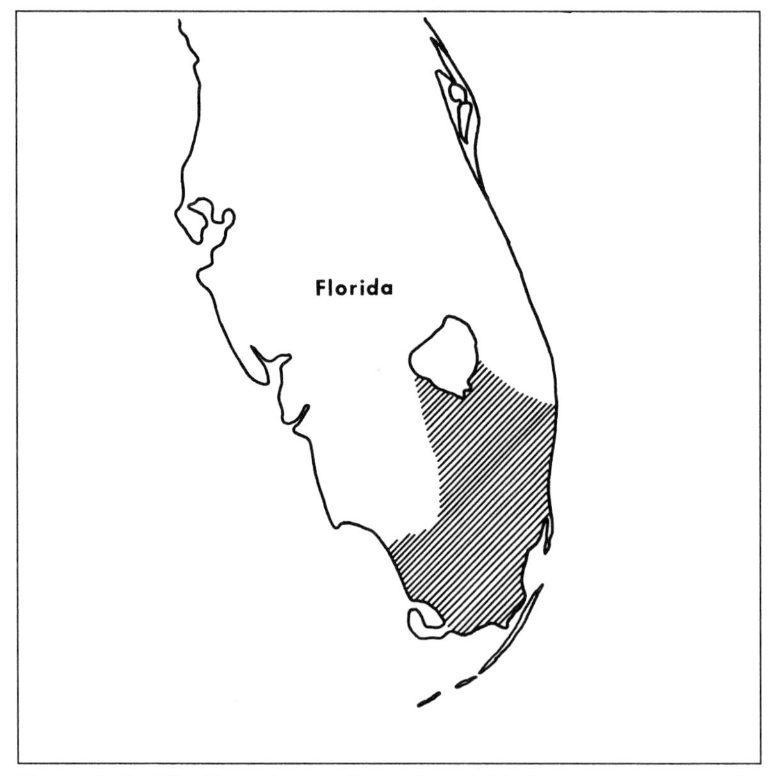

Figure 9–9 The Everglades of southeast Florida are being rapidly modified by human activities.

rapidly modified by human activities. Diking and filling of wetlands have eliminated habitats of fish and waterfowl. The introduction of exotic species has transformed the composition of aquatic communities. The reduction of freshwater inflow for reservoirs has changed the dynamics of plant and animal communities of the wetlands. In addition, urban and industrial wastes have contaminated sediments as well as organisms. The continued disposal of toxic wastes and the further reduction of freshwater inflows continue to alter wetland water quality and biological communities.

The world's wetlands are often drained to provide additional farmland. Nearly 90 percent of recent wetland loss in the United States has been for agricultural purposes. Woodland marshes are disappearing at the alarming rate of over 1,000 acres a day. As sea levels continue to rise due to higher global temperatures, 80 percent of the U.S. coastal wetlands and estuaries could be lost by the middle of the next century.

The urgent need to feed growing populations is the major reason developing countries drain wetlands. Short-term food production has obscured the long-term economic and ecologic benefits of preserving wetland habi-

Figure 9–10a A fringing coral reef in Puerto Rico. Photo by C. A. Kaye, courtesy of USGS

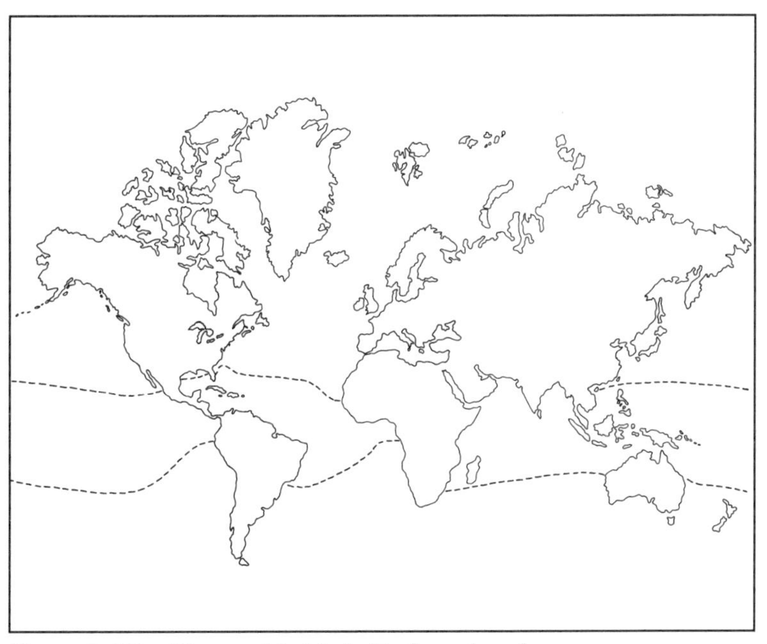

Figure 9–10b The worldwide belt of coral reefs.

tats. The disappearance of the wetlands is responsible for the loss of local fisheries and breeding grounds for marine species and wildlife. In many cases, wetland destruction is irreversible.

Coral reefs (Figs. 9-10a&b) are also centers of high biological productivity, and their fisheries provide a major food source for the tropical regions. Unfortunately, the spread of tourist resorts along coral coasts in many parts of the world harms the productivity of these areas. Such developments are almost always accompanied by increased sewage dumping, overfishing, and physical damage to the reef by construction, dredging, dumping, and landfilling. Reefs are also destroyed to provide tourists with curios and souvenirs. In addition, upland deforestation chokes off coral reefs with eroded sediment dumped into the water by rivers.

In many areas, such as Bermuda, the Virgin Islands, and Hawaii, urban development and sewage outflows have led to extensive overgrowth by thick mats of algae that suffocate and eventually kill the coral by supporting the growth of oxygen-consuming bacteria. The reefs are particularly at risk during the winter, when the algal cover on shallow reefs is extensive (Fig. 9-11), resulting in the loss of living coral and the eventual destruction of the reef by erosion.

Figure 9–11 The algal zone of a reef fringing Agana Bay, on the island of Guam.
Photo by J. I. Tracey, Jr., courtesy of USGS

Figure 9–12 Foraminifera are marine plankton that play important roles in the global carbon cycle and food chains.

Increasing ocean temperatures cause the bleaching of many reefs, turning corals deathly white due to the expulsion of symbiotic (helpful) algae from their tissues. The algae aid in nourishing the corals, and their loss poses a great danger to the reefs. Foraminifera (Fig. 9-12), which are marine plankton and are important players in the global carbon cycle and food chain, are suffering from a similar bleaching effect.

Acid rain is a growing threat to the environment. It is especially harmful to aquatic organisms, and most species cannot tolerate high acidity levels in their environments. In seawater, the damage is due to nitrogen oxides in acid rain. Nitrogen is a nutrient that promotes the growth of floating algae, which blocks sunlight and halts photosynthesis below the ocean surface. When the algae die and decompose, bacteria deplete the water of its dissolved oxygen, which in turn suffocates other aquatic plants and animals.

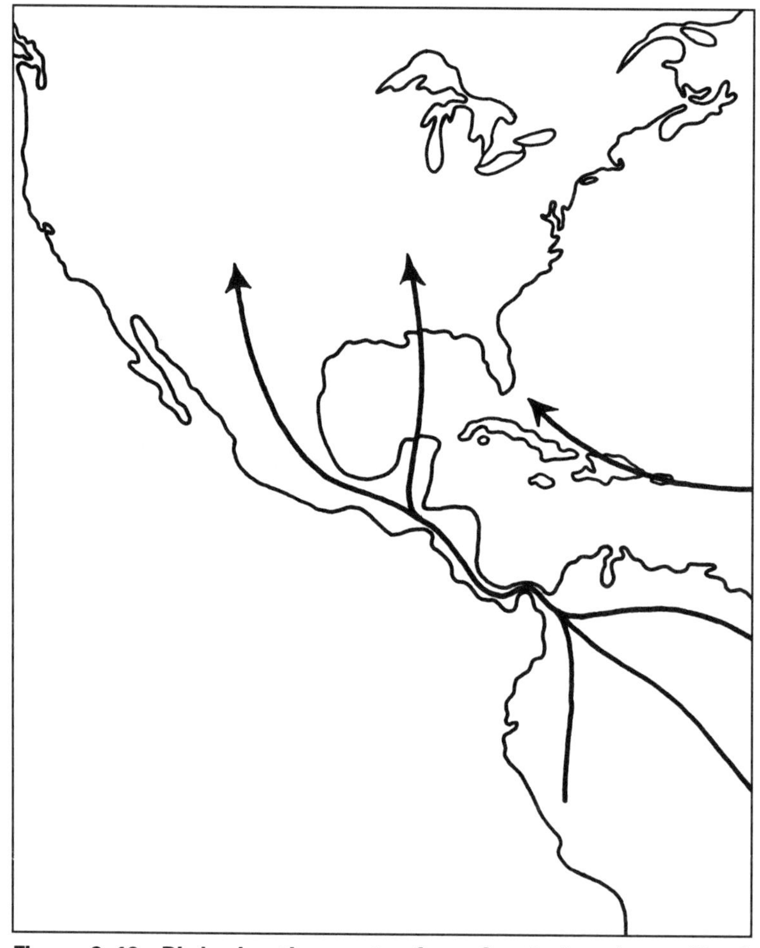

Figure 9–13 Bird migration routes from South America to North America.

In addition to nitrogen oxides, the ocean is contaminated from widespread increases in nitrate levels along with higher concentrations of toxic metals, including arsenic, cadmium, and selenium. The main factors contributing to these increases are fertilizer, herbicide, and pesticide runoff along with acid rain, which dissolves heavy metals in the soil. Moreover, riverine fisheries have been damaged by increased sedimentation from erosion and deforestation in catchment areas that supply water for rivers and aquifers.

Tropical rain forests in Africa and the New World have been dramatically reduced. These rain forests are the wintering grounds for migratory birds from the Northern Hemisphere (Fig. 9-13). The numbers of ducks and other waterfowl there have fallen drastically due to the drainage of wetlands where they breed. The disappearance of the rain forests could mean silent springs for the northern regions. Already birds are disappearing in alarming numbers, and like canaries used for detecting poisonous gas in coal mines, they could be sounding a quiet warning that the planet is in trouble.

Birds are not the only species in trouble. The African elephant and the black rhinoceros, along with other large mammals, are in danger of extinction due to a greedy ivory trade and human encroachment into their habitats. These large herbivores improve their environment by opening forests for grass undergrowth, which increases productivity and accelerates nutrient recycling. Unfortunately, with the elimination of these animals, their favorable environmental impacts are reversed, restricting the habitats of smaller herbivores, which follow their larger cohabitants into extinction.

SPECIES DIVERSITY

The human race came into existence during the greatest period of biological diversity in the history of the planet, when nearly three-quarters of today's species evolved. We have been blessed with a highly diverse and interesting biosphere, filled with more species than have existed during any other period of geologic time. As human populations continue to expand and to alter the natural environment, however, they are reducing biological diversity to its lowest level since the great extinction of the dinosaurs and 70 percent of all other known species 65 million years ago.

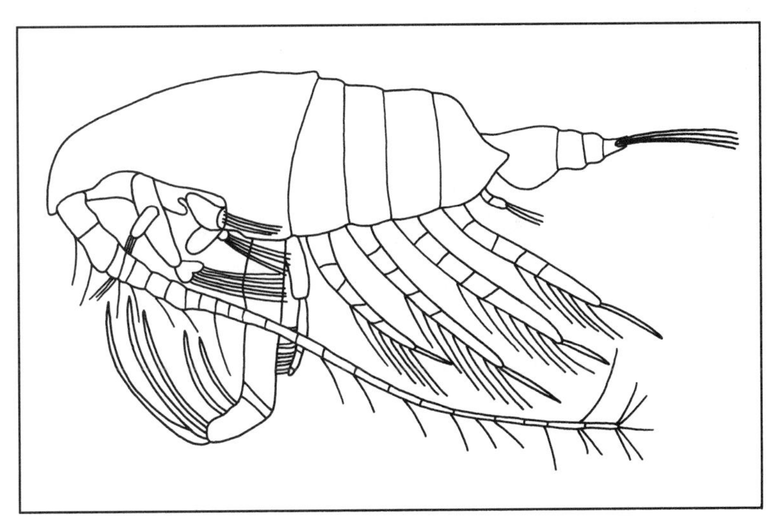

Figure 9–14 Tiny organisms like this krill provide food for larger species.

Extremes in climate and topography during the Cenozoic, the era that followed the age of the dinosaurs, produced a greater variety of living conditions than any other equivalent span of Earth history. The rigorous environments presented many challenging opportunities, and the extent to which plants and animals invaded diverse habitats was truly remarkable. The invasion of new habitats, in which repopulation occurs following a major extinction, is the major source of evolutionary opportunities. As a response to those opportunities, species show a burst of evolutionary development that gives rise to great diversity.

Perhaps as many as 4 billion species have inhabited the Earth throughout all of geologic time. The number of species today ranges from 5 million to as many as 30 million. Only about 1.4 million species have been formally classified, however. Most species go about their lives completely unnoticed. Many small organisms play critical roles in food chains and make important nutrients available to higher organisms. These simple creatures, including bacteria, fungi, and plankton (Fig. 9-14), comprise 80 percent or

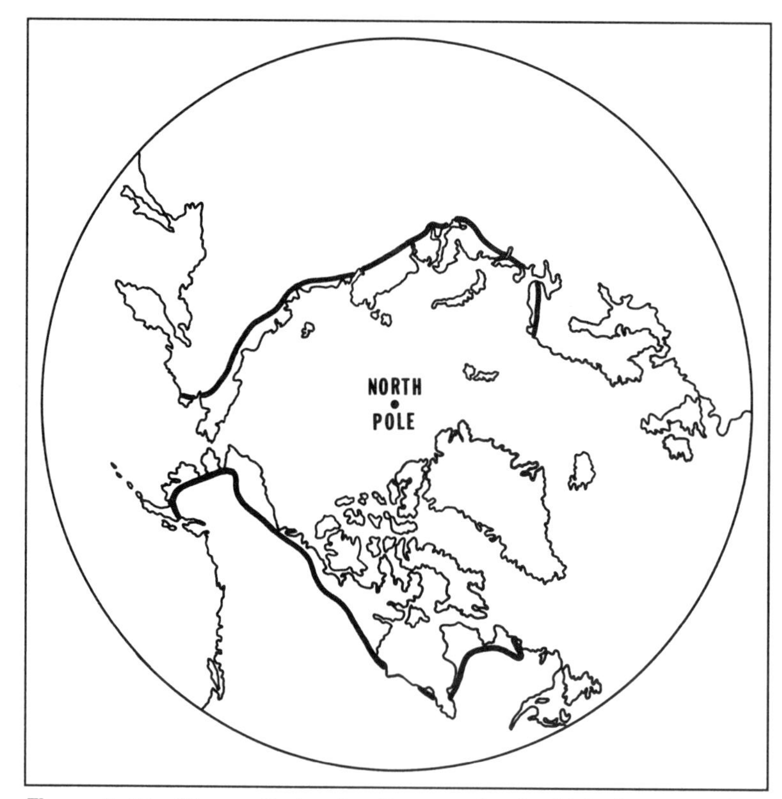

Figure 9–15 The arctic tundra line, north of which the ground remains frozen year-round.

more of the Earth's biomass. Moreover, marine phytoplankton produce most of the breathable oxygen available on the planet. These are the organisms that hold nature in balance; as they go, so go humans.

In the past, climate changes were slow enough to allow the biological world to adapt. But today's climate changes are more abrupt, perhaps abrupt enough to cause the extinction of plants and animals. Plants would be the species hardest hit by global warming, because they are directly affected by changes in temperature and rainfall. Forests, especially game preserves, might become isolated from their normal climate conditions, and would continue to move to higher latitudes. Human intervention on an unprecedented scale might be required to preserve plant and animal species threatened by climate change, especially if it is rapid.

The effects of global climate change with increasing temperatures and rainfall would be felt for centuries, during which time forests would creep poleward, while other wildlife habitats, including the arctic tundra (Fig. 9-15), would disappear. Many species would be unable to keep pace with these rapid climate changes, and those that were able to migrate could find their routes blocked by natural and man-made barriers, such as cities and farms. The warming would rearrange entire biological communities, causing many species to become extinct, while allowing pests to overrun the landscape.

High levels of carbon dioxide, a gas that functions like a fertilizer, favor the growth of weeds. The warmer climate would be a boon for parasites and pathogens, including bacteria and viruses, and could cause an influx of tropical diseases into the temperate zone. The culminating effect would be diminished species diversity worldwide, which could adversely affect humans as well. If the number of species continues to decline because of human interference with their habitats, our own species might well be next in line.

10

THE HABITABILITY CRISIS

If science and technology can put a man on the moon (Fig. 10-1), why can't they correct the multitude of problems we have inflicted on our planet? This is a commonly asked question—but scientists themselves have few answers. When the world is filled with too many people, technology can no longer solve our problems but can only postpone them, leaving future generations to deal with the repercussions.

Modern technology can, however, provide the tools of measurement and computation to study the Earth as a complete system. Scientists have gained a comprehensive knowledge of the state of the planet and of its global processes. They also have become uncomfortably aware that major changes are taking place and that our species is responsible for serious disruptions to the planet we live on.

OVERCROWDING

The environmental problems that plague our world will need to be solved in the very near future. If we wait too long, corrective actions could well be of little use. The world's problems are growing exponentially as human populations are exploding. Our excess numbers are overloading both the

Figure 10–1 Astronaut Edwin E. Aldrin, Jr. walking on the lunar surface. Courtesy of NASA

environment and human communities. Overcrowding is wrecking the very fabric of society, contributing to unemployment, lawlessness, homelessness, and a host of other social ills worldwide.

Overcrowded cities are vulnerable to natural disasters. Earthquakes take the lives of a great many people, as buildings topple down on them (Fig. 10-2). People crowding into coastal regions and low-lying river deltas are particularly at risk from tropical storms (Fig. 10-3). Population growth in the past few decades has pushed people closer to the world's 600 active volcanoes (Fig. 10-4). During this century, volcanoes have killed about 1,000 people annually, a number that is bound to rise as populations living

Figure 10–2 Rubble from a brick building that completely collapsed during the July 28, 1976, Tangsham, China earthquake, which killed a quarter of a million people. Courtesy of USGS

Figure 10–3 Overwash damage from storm surge at Cape Hatteras, North Carolina in 1962. Photo by R. Dolan, courtesy of USGS

Figure 10–4 The June 28, 1943 eruption of Parícutin Volcano, Michoacan, Mexico. Photo by W. F. Foshag, courtesy of USGS

near them continue to increase. Aside from the cost in lives, a major natural catastrophe could ruin a nation's economy.

The ideal society attempts to provide its people with the basic requirements of life, including adequate food and shelter along with a healthy environment. Only when these essential needs are met can attention be turned to seeking comfort and convenience, which determines a society's quality of life. Unfortunately, for much of the world, the quality of life suffers as populations continue growing well beyond the capacity of the land to provide for them. As a result, people are forced to spend more time and effort obtaining enough food to stay alive, with little income for improving their standards of living.

A large part of the problem is that societies tend to treat symptoms rather than address the main issue, which is our staggering population growth. But even when the population remains stable, a country that continues to try to improve its standard of living by making increasing demands on natural resources can be as destructive to the environment as one with a growing population that makes slow increases in living standards. However, slower population growth would allow the human race more time to solve these problems. Population growth can be curbed by lowering birthrates, as China has done, allowing only one child per family. Growth is also slowed when death rates rise, as in many African nations during serious droughts.

Any delays in tackling the many problems brought on by overpopulation would make them practically insurmountable in the future, because mounting volumes of dangerous pollutants, such as those that are destroying the ozone layer, remain in the environment for a long time. Furthermore, the loss of wildlife habitats such as rain forests and the plant and animal species within them is irreversible. Once a wave of extinction is set in motion, it ultimately undermines the quality or even the possibility of human life.

ECONOMIC DEVELOPMENTS

Rapid population growth has stretched the world's resources, and the prospect of future increases raises serious doubts about whether the planet can continue to support people's growing demands. Up to a tenfold increase in world economic activity over the next 50 years would be required to keep up with basic human needs—a situation the biosphere cannot possibly tolerate without irreversible damage.

Economic developments over large parts of the world are disrupting patterns of land and water use. Global destruction of forests and wildlife habitats, large-scale extraction and combustion of fossil fuels, and widespread use of man-made chemicals in industry and agriculture are permanently altering the cycles of essential nutrients in the biosphere. These activities could also affect the global climate and change precipitation patterns, causing droughts and loss of farm productivity (Fig. 10-5), even as human populations continue to grow.

Humans currently consume directly and indirectly about 4 percent of the terrestrial net primary production, which is the solar energy captured by all land plants. By adding the amount of energy humans waste, the total

Figure 10–5 A dust storm on a farmstead in Baca County, Colorado during the 1930s Dust Bowl years. Here, soil has become airborne, forming clouds of dust so dense that visibility at times is zero and soil drifts around structures. Courtesy of USDA–Soil Conservation Service

rises to nearly 40 percent. The level of human growth over this century alone has been staggering. At the present rate of growth, the population is expected to double by the middle of the 21st century, and humans would thus require twice the present consumption of the world's net primary production. This is a preposterous notion considering the destructive impacts of today's level of human activities.

A major part of the problem is that global military expenditures are draining the economies of both large and small countries, preventing them from providing the necessary resources to meet even the most basic human needs. African nations on average spend four times as much money on armaments as on agriculture. For many countries, the true threat to national security is not war but ecological deterioration, which because of expanding human populations is accelerating furiously.

People in many parts of the world are unable to feed themselves properly due to the destruction of their land. The loss of agricultural production is the result of vanishing forests and wetlands, topsoil depletion and desertification, improper irrigation methods and overuse of groundwater, population pressures on limited food and natural resources, and the effects all these interrelated problems have on political and economic stability.

It makes no sense to apply stopgap measures to keep food production in step with growing world populations, while at the same time destroying the very land needed to feed future generations. India, whose population is expected to reach 1 billion by the turn of the century, just manages to feed its citizens. However, it achieved this great feat at the expense of its soil and groundwater by intensive agriculture, thereby making long-term survival doubtful. Each year, the world's farmers must feed an additional 90 million people on 20 billion fewer tons of topsoil. Nations are caught in a dilemma over whether to feed their growing populations today or save the land for tomorrow. Usually, they opt for the first priority, making the future highly uncertain.

Genetic engineering does have a place, however, in agriculture; here it could provide the solution to the problem of worldwide food shortages. Disease- or drought-resistant crop strains are being developed to improve agricultural output, and crops are being genetically engineered to create larger produce. But without being able to afford large quantities of expensive fertilizers to restore the land, and herbicides and pesticides to ward off weeds and pests, the developing countries are still at a disadvantage. Furthermore, the improper use of agricultural chemicals can be exceedingly harmful to the environment. Two or more years of successive drought can wipe out what meager gains are made toward feeding the world's needy, with the additional problem of greater desertification.

Livestock are being genetically engineered to grow rapidly to prodigious sizes, and dairy cows are given growth hormones to increase milk production. Experimenters have proposed that pigs could be given human genes to grow internal organs for transplant operations. Such activities have sparked a scientific and ethical debate over whether these creatures should be altered so that corporations might benefit financially by tinkering with nature.

ENVIRONMENTAL IMPACTS

Environmental degradation in large parts of the world appears to have passed the threshold of irreversibility, meaning that its effects cannot easily be turned around. The degradation of the environment, along with its accompanying threats to health and disruption of ecosystems, is nothing new, however. Human disturbance of the environment has been noted from the earliest recorded history. What is different today is that pollution problems are becoming increasingly obvious, with subtle secondary reverberations that previously went unnoticed , such as runoff from farms killing fish at sea. Moreover, a number of environmental disturbances have begun to manifest themselves on a global scale. Environmental catastrophes are becoming more commonplace as the world's population continues to expand. As with the alarming discovery of the ozone hole over Antarctica, more disturbing surprises loom ahead.

Protecting the environment is becoming exceedingly difficult in the face of the growing global population, the increasing concentrations of populations in cities, and rising standards of living, which rely on large inputs of natural resources. In many parts of the world, environmental protection must yield to economic concerns, such as the threat of lost jobs, bankrupt businesses, and decreased productivity. Cleaning up the environment is an expensive undertaking, and the pursuit of this goal could damage economies through the imposition of heavy taxes.

Figure 10–6 The heavy haze over Zaire, Central Africa created by agricultural burning makes it impossible to see the ground from the space shuttle *Challenger*. Courtesy of NASA

Scientists have good reasons to suspect that increasing human populations are causing changes in today's climate. The famines that frequently ravage Africa are often attributed to drought. But drought might only be part of the problem. The root cause of Africa's crisis is growing population, soil erosion, and desertification, along with tyrannical governments that spend more money on armaments than on feeding their populations.

As developing nations attempt to raise their standards of living, one of the first steps they take is to clear forests and drain wetlands for agriculture. Much of the land is cleared by wasteful slash-and-burn methods (Fig. 10-6), by which forests are set ablaze and the ashes fertilize the thin, nutrient-poor soil. Since artificial fertilizers are expensive and farmers in the developing countries cannot afford them, the soil quickly wears out after a few years of agriculture. The fields are then abandoned, and more forests are put to the torch. The deserted farms are subjected to severe soil erosion due to the loss of vegetative cover that protects against the effects of wind and rain. Once the soil is depleted, rain forests that have existed for 30 million years cannot return.

Soil erosion is without a doubt the greatest limiting factor to further human population growth. As much as one-third of the global cropland is losing soil at a rate that is undermining any long-term agricultural productivity (Fig. 10-7). Natural processes require thousands of years to generate a single inch of topsoil, an amount that is presently being lost worldwide

Figure 10–7 Sheet and rill erosion on this soybean field in Pittsylvania County, Virginia caused soil losses of 80 to 100 tons per acre per year. Photo by T. McCabe, courtesy of USDA–Soil Conservation Service

Figure 10–8 Destruction of Hiroshima, Japan following atomic bombing on August 6, 1945. The Peace Dome in the background remains standing today as a reminder of the horrors of nuclear war. Courtesy of Defense Nuclear Agency

in less than a decade. This situation is particularly distressing since the average soil depth worldwide is only 7 inches. World food production per capita will eventually fall off if the loss of topsoil continues. Short-term efforts to increase crop production to feed bulging populations will ultimately prove self-defeating if in the long run the topsoil erodes away.

The loss of biological diversity, tropical deforestation, forest dieback in the Northern Hemisphere, and climate change are growing geometrically. Unfortunately, these are not perceived as great threats like nuclear war (Fig. 10-8). Therefore, few sacrifices are deemed necessary to forestall the possibility of a global firestorm arising from ecological collapse and its accompanying human misery. Problems such as greenhouse warming, ozone depletion, deforestation, and pollution could, in the long run, pose a greater threat to world peace than the world's militaries.

ECOLOGICAL EFFECTS OF WAR

Overcrowding and growing scarcities of valuable natural resources are contributing to violent conflict in many parts of the world. This condition is especially true for poor countries, where shortages of forests, agricultural land, and water resources, combined with rapidly expanding populations,

are causing unbearable hardships. The supply of advanced weapons to unstable regions, like the Middle East, is not only an impetus to war but makes armed conflicts more violent, resulting in much higher casualties and severe damage to the environment.

The nuclear arsenals of the world are immense and contain a destructive force equivalent to 4 tons of TNT for every man, woman, and child on Earth. The sheer numbers of nuclear weapons reflects an enormous overkill factor, ensuring that nuclear war would make the destruction of the world complete. Therefore, dramatically reducing the stockpiles of nuclear weapons is of utmost importance for the survival of humanity.

The nuclear powers are the United States, Russia, China, Great Britain, and France. Many other nations are believed to be at various stages of nuclear weapons development. They include India, Israel, Egypt, Iraq, Pakistan, South Africa, Brazil, Argentina, and North Korea. One compelling reason for going to war against Iraq in 1991 was to destroy its nuclear and biochemical warfare capability.

Many developing countries that take the nuclear option are poor and politically unstable. The doctrine of deterrence, otherwise known as MAD (for mutual assured destruction), that keeps large nations from annihilating each other might not inhibit aggression by smaller or less developed countries, which have a greater propensity for going to war with their neighbors. Once a developing country possesses a nuclear capability, nearby nations might become militarily insecure and might attempt to obtain nuclear weapons on the black market. When India tested its first nuclear device in 1974, it threatened Pakistan, which attempted to counter this by developing its own nuclear capability at all costs, even though its population was starving.

Some developing countries view biochemical weapons as the "poor man's atomic bomb." Iraq's use of chemical weapons against Iran and its own Kurdish populations during the long Iran-Iraq war of the 1980s demonstrated their availability. Fears that Iraq would unleash its biochemical weapons during the 1991 Persian Gulf war heightened preparations to safeguard Allied soldiers and civilian populations in the affected areas. During the war and its aftermath, the Allies destroyed much of Iraq's capacity to further threaten the region with weapons of mass destruction.

Since 1980, the United States has indulged in biological and chemical weapons research, despite a 1972 treaty banning the production and stockpiling of these terrible weapons for offensive use. A mysterious epidemic that killed over 1,000 people in the Russian city of Sverdlovsk in 1979 was believed to have been caused by anthrax bacteria developed for germ warfare and accidentally released during an explosion at a nearby military laboratory. The use in war of genetically engineered microbes, against which the body has no natural immunities, would be the most horrible action humans could take against their fellow humans.

TABLE 10–1 EFFECTS OF RADIATION

Dose (in rems)	Immediate Effects	Long-term Effects	Comments
0–50	No apparent injury Chromosome change	Genetic damage	Can cause birth defects and later cancers
50–100	Minor vomiting, depressed blood count, malaise, slight fatigue	Genetic damage	Symptoms begin in a few hours and may last a day or more
100–200	Vomiting more common, loss of appetite, sore throat, thirst, fever, minor diarrhea	Symptoms may reappear in two or three weeks	Fewer than 5% will die from radiation sickness
200–300	Above symptoms more pronounced, greater fatigue, sterility in both sexes	Gum, intestinal and skin bleeding, loss of hair, depletion of white blood cells causes infection	20% of the population will die within two weeks
300–400	Symptoms more severe and occur more rapidly, most victims require clinical treatment	Gastrointestinal disorders, kidney bleeding, loss of hair, leukemia and thyroid cancer	Death from dehydration and starvation, up to seven-week hospital stay
400–500	Same as above only worse, all victims require clinical treatment	Skin burn and skin cancer, extensive internal bleeding, gastric ulcers, liver and lung disease	50% fatality rate, death in one month, ten-week hospital stay
500–1000	Generally fatal, severe illness, vomiting will continue for several days, intense cramps and bloody diarhhea	Permanent sterility and loss of hair, cataracts, intense ulceration, nerve disorders, pneumonia	100% fatality rate without intense clinical treatment, extreme agony, death in two weeks
Over 1000	Victim will go into spasms and convulsions, death in one to two days	None	Virtually all die, onset of coma within a few hours

It has been predicted that the immediate casualties of global nuclear and biochemical warfare would involve half or more of the total human population. Not only would people die in tragically large numbers, but most species of plants and animals would be killed as well. Diseases would spread in epidemic proportions from decomposed, unburied human and animal corpses. Radioactive fallout along with acids and poisons would contaminate the soil and water, killing off microorganisms that are beneficial to plants and aquatic species, thereby disrupting entire food chains. The cold and dark resulting from dust and soot clogging the atmosphere would halt photosynthesis and cause a cataclysmic collapse of life support systems. Besides toxic chemicals generated by burning cities, the specter of chemical and biological weapons used along with nuclear weapons would make survival for all Earth's inhabitants nearly impossible.

Even conventional warfare is extremely destructive to the environment. During the 1991 Persian Gulf War, the Iraqis deliberately dumped over a million barrels of crude oil into the Persian Gulf. This terrorist act threatened to cause unprecedented damage to the ecology of the region for some time. In the wake of their retreat from Kuwait, the Iraqis set fire to over 500 Kuwaiti oil wells, blackening the skies with thick clouds of soot and turning day into dusk. The smoke emissions, the worst ever recorded, caused severe and deadly pollution in Kuwait. It was the worst environmental catastrophe in modern history.

THE PEOPLE PROBLEM

The world's biggest problem is a people problem. Our species appears to be responsible for many of the environmental woes that beset the Earth. The growing number of humans is often missing, however, from the debate on the deteriorating condition of the planet. This encompasses global warming, pollution, acid precipitation, ozone depletion, deforestation, desertification, species extinction, and a host of other serious problems that are exacerbated by growing human populations.

The human race is being squeezed between limited resources and the growing numbers of people using them. Rapid population growth has stretched the resources of the world, and the prospect of future increases raises serious doubts whether the planet is capable of supporting people's growing demands. The level of human growth over this century has been staggering, and could be disastrous, considering the destructive impacts of today's level of human activities (Fig. 10-9).

Every added ton of carbon dioxide, every additional gallon of pollution, and every species extinction brings the world closer to a habitability crisis. With more people in the world, more forests are cleared, more firewood is gathered, more topsoil is eroded, and more pollution is generated.

If our understanding of geologic history is accurate, the extinction of large numbers of species is an inevitable occurrence. Human populations are increasing so explosively and modifying the environment so extensively that we are inflicting global damage of unprecedented dimensions, with the potential to cause greater havoc than the worst calamities the planet

Figure 10–9 Burned trees from the 1988 forest fire that devastated Yellowstone National Park. The fire became unmanageable during a controlled burn in a severe drought. Courtesy of National Park Service

has ever endured. Possibly by the middle of the next century, the number of extinct species could exceed those lost in the great extinctions of the geologic past. Plants and animals are forced into extinction as growing human populations continue to squander the Earth's space and resources and contaminate the soil, water, and air. The extinction of large numbers of species is comparable to popping rivets on Spaceship Earth. Eventually, it will all fall apart.

We have yet to feel the adverse effects of such a large die-out of species. But this situation could quickly change as species continue to disappear. If the present spiral of human population and environmental destruction continues out of control, the Earth's biological support systems might begin to fail. It would be a great tragedy if through our neglect of the environment and wanton destruction of life, we were to so perturb the planet as to return it to a condition of low diversity. The human race would then lose the great beauty and wonder of this planet (Fig. 10-10) and jeopardize the future for generations of humankind.

Figure 10–10 The snow-covered peaks of the Rocky Mountains near Telluride, Colorado. Photo by W. Cross, courtesy of USGS

GLOSSARY

abyss — the deep ocean, generally over a mile in depth

acid precipitation — any type of precipitation with abnormally high levels of sulfuric and nitric acids

aerosol — a mass made of solid or liquid particles dispersed in air

air pollution — the contamination of air by industrial and automobile exhaust

albedo — the amount of light reflected by an object; often refers specifically to sunlight reflected off the Earth's surface

alluvium — stream-deposited sediment

alpine glacier — a mountain glacier or a glacier in a mountain valley

anaerobic — occurring in the absence of oxygen

aquifer — a subterranean bed of sediments through which groundwater flows

atmosphere — a thin membrane of gases surrounding the Earth, divided into the troposphere, which ranges from zero to 10 miles altitude and comprises 80 percent of the air mass, and the stratosphere, which ranges from 10 to 40 miles altitude and contains low-pressure stable air

barrier island — a low, elongated coastal island that parallels the shoreline and protects the beach from storms

bicarbonate	an ion created by the action of carbonic acid on surface rocks. Organisms use the bicarbonate along with calcium to build supporting structures composed of calcium carbonate
biochemical warfare	the use of biological and chemical agents as weapons of war
biodegradable	capable of being broken down into environmentally safe substances by the action of living organisms
biogenic	sediments composed of the remains of plant and animal life, such as shells
biosphere	the living portion of the Earth that interacts with all other geological and biological processes
calving	formation of icebergs by ice breaking off glaciers upon entering the ocean
carbonaceous	containing carbon; a property of sedimentary rocks such as limestone and certain types of meteorites
carbonate	a mineral containing calcium carbonate, such as limestone and dolostone
carbon cycle	the flow of carbon into the atmosphere and ocean, its conversion to carbonate rock, and its subsequent return to the atmosphere by volcanoes
carcinogen	any natural or man-made substance that causes cancer
carrying capacity	the maximum number of organisms a habitat can support
catchment area	an area that contributes groundwater to an aquifer, or water-filled rock
chlorofluorocarbon	a compound that contains carbon, chlorine, fluorine, and sometimes hydrogen, used in a variety of manufacturing processes and blamed for the destruction of the upper atmospheric ozone layer
climate	the average course of the weather over time for a certain region
coal	a fossil fuel deposit originating from metamorphosed plant material that contains significant quantities of

	carbon; when ignited, coal releases more carbon dioxide than other fossil fuels
coastal storm	a cyclonic low-pressure system moving along a coastal plain or just offshore
cogeneration	the simultaneous generation of electricity and heat from a single source of energy
community	a self-sustaining environment composed of a variety of organisms
conservation	the preservation and protection of a natural resource
contaminant	any substance that pollutes the environment
continental glacier	an ice sheet covering a portion of a continent
continental shelf	the offshore area of a continent in shallow sea
continental slope	the transition from the continental margin to the deep sea basin
contraception	the act of deliberately preventing pregnancy
convection	a circular, vertical flow of a fluid medium due to heating from below. As materials are heated, they become less dense and rise, while cooler, heavier materials sink
coral	any of a large group of shallow-water, bottom-dwelling marine invertebrates, that commonly build reef colonies in warm waters
deforestation	the clearing of forests for agriculture and other purposes
desertification	the process by which land becomes barren through natural processes or through mismanagement
deterrence	a strategic doctrine for the prevention of war by the buildup of arms
developed nation	a heavily industrialized, generally rich country
developing nation	a generally poor country that is beginning to industrialize
diversification	a wide variety of species

drought	a period of abnormally dry weather sufficiently prolonged for the lack of water to cause serious deleterious effects on agricultural and other biological activities
dune	a ridge of wind-blown sediments, usually in motion
earthquake	the sudden breaking of the Earth's crust by tectonic forces
ecology	the interrelationship between organisms and their environment
ecosphere	the complex interconnections between the biosphere, hydrosphere, atmosphere, and lithosphere
ecosystem	a community of organisms and their environment that functions as a complete, self-contained biological unit
effluent	an outflow of liquid waste material, usually considered a pollutant
El Niño	an anomalous ocean warming in the southeast Pacific
endangered species	a species threatened with extinction
environment	the complex physical and biological factors that act on an organism to determine its survival and evolution
erosion	the wearing away of surface materials by natural agents such as wind and water
estuary	tidal inlet along a coast; an important environment for fish and shellfish
evaporation	the transformation of a liquid into a gas
evaporite	a mineral deposit derived from the evaporation of a brine
evolution	the tendency of physical and biological factors to change with time
exponential growth	a total amount or number compounded by a certain yearly percentage, such as compound interest at a bank; at an annual human growth rate of about 1.7 percent, a population of five billion people in 1987 would double by about the year 2030

extinction	the elimination of a species
famine	the mass starvation of people
floodplain	the land adjacent to a watercourse that can flood during river overflows
fluvial deposit	sedimentary material deposited by a river, especially during floods.
fossil fuel	an energy source derived from ancient plant and animal life; includes coal, oil, and natural gas. When ignited, these fuels release carbon dioxide stored in the Earth's crust for millions of years
genetic engineering	the manipulation of genes to induce certain characteristics in an organism
geologic column	the total thickness of geologic units in a region
geothermal	relating to the movement of hot water through the Earth's crust; geothermal energy is an important renewable energy source
glacier	a thick mass of moving ice occurring where winter snowfall exceeds summer melting
greenhouse effect	the trapping of heat in the atmosphere, principally by water vapor, carbon dioxide, and methane
groundwater	the water derived from the atmosphere that percolates and circulates below the surface
habitat	the environment in which organisms live
hazardous waste	any pollutant that is particularly harmful to life, including toxic substances and nuclear wastes
heat budget	the flow of solar energy through the atmosphere, onto the surface of the Earth, and back out into space
hydrocarbon	a molecule consisting of carbon chains with attached hydrogen atoms
hydrologic cycle	the flow of water from the sea to the land and back, which plays a major role in cleansing the Earth
hydrosphere	the water layer at the surface of the Earth

hydrothermal vent	a geyser on the deep ocean floor that often supports a community of marine animals
ice age	a period of time when large areas of the Earth were covered by glaciers
iceberg	a portion of a glacier broken off upon entering the sea
ice cap	a polar cover of ice and snow
industrialization	the use of natural resources in manufacturing, transportation, and other human activities
infrared	heat radiation with a wavelength between that of red light and radio waves
insolation	all solar radiation impinging on a planet
interglacial	a warming period between glacial periods
irrigation	an artificial supply of water for agriculture
landfill	a method of municipal solid waste disposal whereby layers of garbage are covered by layers of impermeable clay
landslide	a rapid downhill movement of Earth materials, often triggered by earthquakes
leachate	a solution created by the dissolution of soluble substances such as those found in landfills
limestone	a sedimentary rock consisting mostly of calcite that was deposited as skeletal remains of once-living organisms
lithosphere	the rocky outer layer of the mantle that includes the terrestrial and oceanic crusts. The lithosphere circulates between the Earth's surface and mantle by convection currents
loess	a fine-grained soil deposited during the ice age
mantle	the interior of the Earth between the crust and core
mean temperature	the average of any series of temperatures observed over a period of time
megaherbivore	a large plant-eating animal such as an elephant

metallurgy	a science dealing with metal ores
methane	a hydrocarbon gas liberated by the decomposition of organic matter; a major constituent of natural gas
microorganism	a microscopic plant or animal; also called a microbe
monsoon	a seasonal wind accompanying temperature changes over land and water from one season of the year to another
natural resource	renewable and nonrenewable Earth materials used in industrialization
nitrogen cycle	the cycle by which nitrogen flows from the atmosphere to living organisms, and returns to the atmosphere when the organisms decompose
nitrogen fixation	the readying of nitrogen for plant uptake by root bacteria
nutation	the wobble of the Earth's axis
nutrient	a food substance that nourishes living organisms
oil spill	the dumping of crude oil from all sources on bodies of water, which is harmful to marine life and habitats
oolithic	a sedimentary deposit composed of small, round grains
outgassing	the loss of gas within a planet, as opposed to degassing, which is loss of gas from meteorites
oxygen sink	a substance that removes oxygen from the environment
ozone	a molecule consisting of three atoms of oxygen that exists in the upper atmosphere and filters out ultraviolet light from the sun. Also, a main constituent of urban smog that is extremely toxic
particulate	minute particles of dust or soot dispersed in the atmosphere. Man-made particulates are considered pollution
permafrost	permanently frozen ground in tundra regions
permeability	the ability to transfer fluid through cracks, pores, and interconnected spaces within a rock
petroleum	a hydrocarbon fuel derived from ancient buried microorganisms

pH scale	a logarithmic scale depicting the acidity or alkalinity of a substance, with 0 the strongest acid, 14 the strongest alkaline, and 7 neutral
photochemical reaction	a chemical reaction initiated by sunlight
photosynthesis	the process by which plants create carbohydrates from carbon dioxide, water, and sunlight
phytoplankton	marine or freshwater microscopic single-celled freely drifting plant life
pollutant	any substance that pollutes air or water, whether man-made or natural
precession	the gyration of the Earth's axis
precipitation	products of condensation that fall from clouds as rain, snow, hail, or drizzle
primary producer	the lowest member of a food chain
radioactive waste	nuclear waste products from power plants, weapons manufacture, and hospital laboratories that is classified as hazardous and must be permanently disposed of under special burial conditions
reclamation	a process of restoring an environment to its original condition
reef	the biological community that lives at the edge of an island or continent. The shells form a limestone deposit that is readily preserved in the geologic record.
reserves	known and identified Earth materials for immediate extraction and use
resource	reserves of useful Earth materials that might later be extracted
salinization	the buildup of salts in the soil
saltation	the movement of sand grains by wind or water
sedimentation	the deposition of sediments
soluble	refers to a substance that dissolves in water

storm surge	an abnormal rise of the water level along a shore as a result of wind flow in a storm
stratosphere	the upper atmosphere above the troposphere, from about 10 miles to 40 miles above sea level
surfactant	a surface-active substance on top of a body of water that controls the diffusion of gases and other substances
surge glacier	a continental glacier that heads toward the sea at a high rate of advance during certain periods
temperature inversion	a layer of the atmosphere in which the temperature increases with altitude, opposed to the normal tendency for temperature to decrease with altitude
tide	a bulge in the ocean produced by the moon's gravitational force on the Earth's oceans. The rotation of the Earth beneath this bulge causes the rising and lowering of the sea level
transpiration	the evaporation of water from leaves and other plant parts
troposphere	the lowest 7 to 10 miles of the Earth's atmosphere, where weather occurs
tundra	permanently frozen ground at high latitudes and high altitudes
typhoon	a severe tropical storm in the western Pacific similar to a hurricane
ultraviolet (UV)	the invisible light with a wavelength shorter than visible light and longer than X-rays. There are different kinds of UV light, among them UV-A and UV-B. Most UV-A is unfiltered by the atmosphere and is not harmful. Most UV-B is filtered by the atmosphere and is extremely harmful.
undeveloped nation	a lightly industrialized, usually heavily populated, generally poor country
upwelling	the upward convection of water currents
volcanic ash	fine pyroclastic material injected into the atmosphere by an erupting volcano

volcano	a fissure or vent in the Earth's crust through which molten rock rises to the surface; a major natural source of atmospheric carbon dioxide
water pollution	the contamination of water by industrial and municipal effluents
water vapor	atmospheric moisture in the invisible gaseous phase
wetland	land that is inundated by water and supports a prolific wildlife
zooplankton	small, free-floating or poorly swimming marine or fresh-water animal life

BIBLIOGRAPHY

The Dawn of Civilization

Bar-Yosef, Ofer, and Bernard Vandermeersch. "Modern Humans in the Levant." *Scientific American* 268 (April 1993): 94–100.

Blumenschine, Robert J., and John A. Cavallo. "Scavenging and Human Evolution." *Scientific American* 267 (October 1992): 90–96.

Bower, Bruce. "Erectus Unhinged." *Science News* 141 (June 20, 1992): 408–411.

———. "Neandertals' Disappearing Act." *Science News* 139 (June 8, 1991): 360–363.

Folger, Tim. "The Naked and the Bipedal." *Discover* 14 (November 1993): 34–35.

Putman, John J. "The Search for Modern Humans." *National Geographic* 174 (October 1988): 438–477.

Stringer, Christopher B. "The Emergence of Modern Humans." *Scientific American* 263 (December 1990): 98–103.

Thorne, Alan G., and Milford H. Wolpoff. "The Multiregional Evolution of Humans." *Scientific American* 266 (April 1992): 76–83.

Wilson, Alan C., and Rebecca L. Cann. "The Recent African Genesis of Humans." *Scientific American* 266 (April 1992): 68–73.

The Population Explosion

Berreby, David. "The Numbers Game." *Discover* 11 (April 1990): 43–49.

Caldwell, John C., and Pat Caldwell. "High Fertility in Sub-Saharan Africa." *Scientific American* 263 (May 1990): 118–125.

Demeny, Paul. "World Population Trends." *Current History* 88 (January 1989): 17–19, 58–59, and 64.

Ehrlich, Paul R. "Facing the Habitability Crises." *BioScience* 39 (July/August 1989): 480–482.

Gibbons, Ann. "Pleistocene Population Explosion." *Science* 262 (October 1, 1993): 27–28.

Keyfitz, Nathan. "The Growing Human Population." *Scientific American* 261 (September 1989): 119–135.

Lewin, Roger. "A Revolution of Ideas on Agricultural Origins." *Science* 240 (May 20, 1988): 984–986.

Olshansky, Jay S., Bruce A. Carnes, and Christine K. Cassel. "The Aging of the Human Species." *Scientific American* 268 (April 1993): 46–52.

Percival, Ray. "Malthus and His Ghost." *National Review* 41 (August 18, 1989): 30–33.

Robey, Bryant, Shea O. Rutstein, and Leo Morris. "The Fertility Decline in Developing Countries." *Scientific American* 269 (December 1993): 60–67.

The Balance of Nature

Baskin, Yvonne. "Ecologists Put Some Life into Models of a Changing World." *Science* 259 (March 19, 1993): 1694–1696.

Berner, Robert A., and Antonio C. Lasaga. "Modeling the Geochemical Carbon Cycle." *Scientific American* 260 (March 1989): 74–81.

Green, D. H., S. M. Eggins, and G. Yaxley. "The Other Carbon Cycle." *Nature* 365 (September 16, 1993): 210–211.

Kerr, Richard A. "Ocean-in-a-Machine Starts Looking Like the Real Thing." *Science* 260 (April 2, 1993): 32–33.

———. "No Longer Willful, Gaia Becomes Respectable." *Science* 240 (April 22, 1988): 393–395.

Monastersky, Richard. "The Whole-Earth Syndrome." *Science News* 133 (June 11, 1988): 393–395.

Schell, Jonathan. "Our Fragile Earth." *Discover* 10 (October 1989): 45–50.

Schneider, Stephen H. "Climate Modeling." *Scientific American* 256 (May 1987): 72–80.

Zimmer, Carl. "The Case of the Missing Carbon." *Discover* 14 (December 1993): 38–39.

Environmental Degradation

Goodavage, Maria. "Murky Waters." *Modern Maturity* 32 (August–September 1989): 44–50.

Graedel, Thomas E., and Paul J. Crutzen. "The Changing Atmosphere." *Scientific American* 261 (September 1989): 58–68.

Grossman, Dan, and Seth Hulman. "Down in the Dumps." *Discover* 11 (April 1990): 37–41.

Holloway, Marguerite. "Soiled Shores." *Scientific American* 265 (October 1991): 103–116.

Mohnen, Volker A. "The Challenge of Acid Rain." *Scientific American* 259 (August 1988): 30–38.

O'Leary, Philip R., Patrick W. Walsh, and Robert K. Ham. "Managing Solid Waste." *Scientific American* 259 (December 1988): 36–42.

Pfeiffer, Beth. "Our Disposable Society." *American Legion Magazine* (January 1990): 24–25 and 58.

Raloff, Janet. "Mercurial Risks from Acid's Reign." *Science News* 139 (March 9, 1991): 152–156.

la Riviere, J. W. Maurits. "Threats to the World's Water." *Scientific American* 261 (September 1989): 80–94.

Stolarski, Richard S. "The Antarctic Ozone Hole." *Scientific American* 258 (January 1988): 30–36.

Zimmer, Carl. "Son of Ozone Hole." *Discover* 14 (October 1993): 28–29.

Resource Depletion

Abelson, Philip H. "Increased Use of Renewable Energy." *Science* 253 (September 1991): 1073.

Davis, Ged R. "Energy for Planet Earth." *Scientific American* 263 (September 1990): 55–62.

Fulkerson, William, Roddie R. Judkins, and Manoj K. Sanghvi. "Energy from Fossil Fuels." *Scientific American* 263 (September 1990): 129–135.

Gibbons, John H., Peter D. Blair, and Holly L. Gwin. "Strategies for Energy Use." *Scientific American* 261 (September 1989): 136–143.

Hapgood, Fred. "The Quest for Oil." *National Geographic* 176 (August 1989): 226–263.

Hubbard, Harold M. "The Real Cost of Energy." *Scientific American* 264 (April 1991): 36–42.

Kerr, Richard A. "Geothermal Tragedy of the Commons." *Science* 253 (July 12, 1991): 134–135.

Repetto, Robert. "Accounting for Environmental Assets." *Scientific American* 266 (June 1992): 94–100.

Rosenfield, Arthur H., and David Hafemeister. "Energy-efficient Buildings." *Scientific American* 258 (April 1988): 78–85.

Climate Change

Horgan, John. "Arctic Meltdown." *Scientific American* 268 (March 1993): 19–28.

Jones, Philip D., and Tom M. L. Wigley. "Global Warming Trends." *Scientific American* 263 (August 1990): 84–91.

Maslin, Mark. "Waiting for the Polar Meltdown." *New Scientist* 139 (September 4, 1993): 36–41.

Monastersky, Richard. "Time for Action." *Science News* 139 (March 31, 1991): 200–202.

———. "Global Change: The Scientific Challenge." *Science News* 135 (April 15, 1989): 232–235.

Pollack, Henry N., and David S. Chapman. "Underground Records of Changing Climate." *Scientific American* 268 (June 1993): 44–50.

Ramanathan, V. "The Greenhouse Theory of Climate Change: A Test by Inadvertent Global Experiment." *Science* 240 (April 15, 1988): 293–299.

Revkin, Andrew C. "Endless Summer: Living with the Greenhouse Effect." *Discover* 9 (October 1988): 50–61.

Schneider, Stephen H. "The Changing Climate." *Scientific American* 261 (September 1989): 70–79.

———. "The Greenhouse Effect: Science and Policy." *Science* 243 (February 1989): 771–779.

White, Robert. "The Great Climate Debate." *Scientific American* 263 (July 1990): 36–43.

Carrying Capacity

Crosson, Pierre R., and Norman J. Rosenberg. "Strategies for Agriculture." *Scientific American* 261 (September 1989): 128–135.

Madeley, John. "Will Rice Turn the Sahel to Salt?" *New Scientist* 140 (October 9, 1993): 35–37.

Pennisi, Elizabeth. "Dancing Dust." *Science News* 142 (October 3 1992): 218–220.

Raloff, Janet. "Holding on to the Earth." *Science News* 126 (October 30, 1993): 280–281.

Reganold, John P., Robert I. Papendick, and James F. Parr. "Sustainable Agriculture." *Scientific American* 262 (June 1990): 112–120.

Rosenberg, A. A., et al. "Achieving Sustainable Use of Renewable Resources." *Science* 262 (November 5, 1993): 828–829.

Sen, Amartya. "The Economics of Life and Death." *Scientific American* 268 (May 1993): 40–47.

Tangley, Laura. "Preparing for Climate Change." *BioScience* 38 (January 1988): 14–18.

HABITAT DESTRUCTION

Booth, William. "Monitoring the Fate of the Forests from Space." *Science* 243 (March 17, 1989): 1428–1429.

Cohn, Jeffrey P. "Gauging the Biological Impacts of the Greenhouse Effect." *BioScience* 39 (March 1989): 142–146.

Colinvaux, Paul A. "The Past and Future Amazon." *Scientific American* 260 (May 1989): 102–108.

Goulding, Michael. "Flooded Forests of the Amazon." *Scientific American* 266 (March 1993): 114–120.

Ellis, William S. "Brazil's Imperiled Rain Forest." *National Geographic* 174 (December 1988): 772–799.

Monastersky, Richard. "The Deforestation Debate." *Science News* 144 (July 10, 1993): 26–27.

———. "Climate Influence on Forest Fires." *Science News* 134 (July 23, 1988): 55.

Repetto, Robert. "Deforestation in the Tropics." *Scientific American* 262 (April 1990): 36–42.

Revkin, Andrew. "Cooling Off the Greenhouse." *Discover* 10 (January 1989): 30–33.

Stewart, Doug. "Green Giants." *Discover* 11 (April 1990): 61–64.

BIOLOGICAL EXTINCTION

Barinaga, Marcia. "Where Have All the Froggies Gone?" *Science* 247 (March 2, 1990): 1033–1034.

Brown, Barbara E., and John C. Ogden. "Coral Bleaching." *Scientific American* 268 (January 1993): 64–70.

Diamond, Jared. "Playing Dice With Megadeath." *Discover* 11 (April 1990): 55–59.

Ehrlich, Paul R., and Edward O. Wilson. "Biodiversity Studies: Science and Policy." *Science* 253 (August 16, 1991): 758–761.

Grove, Richard H. "Origin of Western Environmentalism." *Scientific American* 267 (July 1992): 42–47.

Kunzig, Robert. "Invisible Garden." *Discover* 11 (April 1990): 67–74.

May, Robert M. "How Many Species Inhabit the Earth?" *Scientific American* 267 (October 1992): 42–48.

Myers, Norman. "Extinction Rates Past and Present." *BioScience* 39 (January 1989): 39–40.

Roberts, Leslie. "Extinction Imminent for Native Plants." *Science* 242 (December 16, 1988): 1508.

Terborgh, John. "Why American Songbirds Are Vanishing." *Scientific American* 266 (May 1992): 98–104.

Wilson, Edward O. "Threats to Biodiversity." *Scientific American* 261 (September 1989): 108–116.

The Habitability Crisis

Bouvier, Leon F. "How to Get There from Here: Achieving Optimal Population Size." *USA Today* 119 (January 1991): 17–19.

Clark, William C. "Managing Planet Earth." *Scientific American* 261 (September 1989): 47–54.

Franklin, Deborah. "The Successful Animal." *Science 86* 7 (January/February 1986): 55–59.

Holden, Constance. "A Revisionist Look at Population and Growth." *Science* 231 (March 28, 1986): 1493–1494.

Homer-Dixon, Thomas F., Jeffrey H. Boutwell, and George W. Rathjens. "Environmental Change and Violent Conflict." *Scientific American* 268 (February 1993): 38–45.

Lovejoy, Thomas E. "Will Unexpectedly the Top Blow Off?" *BioScience* 38 (November 1988): 722–726.

MacNeill, Jim. "Strategies for Sustainable Economic Development." *Scientific American* 261 (September 1989): 155–165.

Ruckelshaus, William D. "Toward a Sustainable World." *Scientific American* 261 (September 1989): 166–174.

Tilling, Robert I., and Peter W. Lipman. "Lessons in Reducing Volcano Risk." *Nature* 364 (July 22, 1993): 277–280.

INDEX

Italic page numbers indicate illustrations or captions. Page numbers followed by m indicate maps; t indicate tables; g indicate glossary.

B